MY DREAM HUNT IN ALASKA

STEVE CHAPMAN

HARVEST HOUSE PUBLISHERS
EUGENE, OREGON

All Scripture quotations are taken from the New American Standard Bible®, © 1960, 1962, 1963, 1968, 1971, 1972, 1973, 1975, 1977, 1995 by The Lockman Foundation. Used by permission. (www.Lockman.org)

Cover by Bryce Williamson

Cover photos © shaunl, Kaido KArner, Keith Binns, RTsubin, Earl Eliason / Signature collection / iStock

Interior photos by Lindsey Williams

Surveyor *anchored photos by Dale Adams*

Fur-Fish-Game *cover image courtesy of* FFG *editor Mitchell Cox*

MY DREAM HUNT IN ALASKA

Published by Harvest House Publishers
Eugene, Oregon 97402
www.harvesthousepublishers.com

ISBN 978-0-7369-6885-0 (pbk.)
ISBN 978-0-7369-6887-4 (eBook)

Printed in the United States of America

16 17 18 19 20 21 22 23 24 / VP-CD / 10 9 8 7 6 5 4 3 2 1

To the man who was there to guide me
when I went hunting for truth.
He led me to the trophy of God's grace.
That man was my dad,
Paul J. Chapman.

Paul J. Chapman

Contents

Embracing the Dream

Hunters are thinkers. We think about yesterday, perhaps recalling times when we were in the woods with a loved one or a dear friend, wishing it could happen again. Or we remember past encounters with animals, pondering what we did right or wrong during the hunt and how we can apply the lessons we've learned.

We think about today. In the moments when we exit our vehicles to go to a favorite hunting place, we check the wind and consider how it might affect an approach to a field or a patch of woods. During the vigil, our eyes continuously feed information to our minds as we scan an area for movement and changes in shapes and colors. Our ears monitor sounds to determine their cause. We look at the next hill and wonder what we'll see when we top the ridge and peek over. We think about what's in the next meadow.

We think about tomorrow. We quietly plan where we'll be hunting when morning comes, what time we need to leave the house in order to be settled in our blinds before the sun rises. We calculate to the second how late we can stay out the next day and still make it back home without getting in trouble with our families.

In addition to thinking about yesterday, today, and tomorrow, many of us are dreamers. We look way out into the future and see ourselves someday walking in a place where we've never hunted, going after an animal we've seen only in photos or videos. In our imagination, we have our backpacks strapped on, bows in hand or guns on our shoulders. We're glassing, stalking, moving in for the shot across terrain that's vastly different from where we usually engage in the fair chase. The very thought of it is thrilling, and we wonder what it would be like to live it for real.

I have dreams like that. And gratefully, I lived to see one of the special ones come true. The place in my dream was far, far away from the hills of West Virginia where I'd first hunted. I'd heard that the special land is incredibly beautiful, unbelievably massive, and perfect for an adventure of a lifetime. Where did I long to go? Alaska.

The beast in my imagined hunt was the mighty brown bear, an animal of massive size that fits its huge home territory. People told me that the brown dominates all other wild residents in his world and intimidates invading humans so much that few dare enter his domain without utmost respect for his strength. What could be more exciting?

In my dream, I'm not hunting alone. With me is an expert guide because, according to the stories I read when I was a young buck, venturing into big bear country alone for the first time—or anytime for that matter—would not be wise.

I'm grateful you've chosen to take the journey to the Last Frontier with me. Our adventure begins in the Mountaineer State of West Virginia, swings through Tennessee, and then on up to Sitka. A good buddy is going along, and we'll connect with two more friends from the Lower Forty-Eight, meet our very skilled guides, board a big boat, and then sail north through some scenic and remote inland passages.

Let's go!

Alaska, the Last Frontier

1

A Life-Changing Invitation

It was around noon on a Sunday in early October, 1963. Like all the Sundays before, the dismissal prayer was said at the church my dad pastored, and the congregation filed out of the pews and began to mingle. I was thirteen. As I shook a few hands, I had no idea that something was about to happen that would significantly change the course of my life.

Among the attendees was a man named Kenneth Bledsoe. He lived about twelve miles from the town of Point Pleasant, West Virginia, where our church was located. His home sat on a beautiful hilltop along a rural, winding highway that was known as Sand Hill Road. Surrounding his house were hundreds of acres of undeveloped woods and fields. He owned a few acres of the land and had access to the other properties. He used them often to feed his intense passion for hunting.

At the time, Kenneth's son, Stephen, had not been born, and he had two daughters who didn't share their dad's interest in the outdoors. Consequently, his desire to pass on the heritage of hunting to a youngster was unfulfilled—that is, until he shook my hand that notable Sunday. As we greeted one another, he posed a question.

"Steve, have you ever been hunting or handled a gun?"

"No, sir." My answer was short on words but long on images that instantly went through my head. The only memory I had of being around any kind of gun was back when I was about seven. I'd stood next to my friend who cried as his dad ripped a Daisy BB gun out of his hands and swung it by the barrel like a baseball bat and wrapped it around a tree in their front yard.

As the rifle broke in half, my friend's dad screamed in rage, "You won't be shooting our chickens again with this thing! Now, go find something else to do."

I shuddered at the momentary recollection of my heartbroken friend and the consequences he'd faced. I waited to hear why Mr. Bledsoe had asked me if I'd ever handled a gun. What followed was an invitation I couldn't accept on the spot even though I wanted to.

"Well, squirrel season is here, and I was wondering if you'd like to join me on a hunt. What do you say?"

With the surprised expression on my face, I must have looked like the youthful city slicker I was. Other than occasionally playing hide-and-seek with a few friends around the brush-lined creek that ran behind our neighborhood, I had very little experience off the concrete. The thought of carrying a real gun with real bullets into the remote wilderness of Mason County caught me off guard.

"I...uh...I...well, I..." I struggled to find an answer that seemed right. I didn't want to disappoint Mr. Bledsoe. After all, he was one of the most beloved men in our church. I finally found the words. "Well, I have to ask my dad first."

Smiling, Mr. Bledsoe let go of my hand. "Give me a call as soon as you know. I have the very gun for you. I'll also supply the shells and even some hunting clothes."

During Sunday lunch, I told my folks about the invitation to go hunting with Mr. Bledsoe. I didn't get an immediate answer—for a very good reason that I wasn't aware of until much later. Dad also had a bad memory of a gun, one that involved his dad.

When Grandpa Chapman was around eight years old, he followed his ten-year-old brother to the barn to get an older brother's shotgun that he'd left there after a morning squirrel hunt. His brother picked up the gun and, thinking it was unloaded, pointed it at Grandpa and jokingly said, "I'm gonna shoot you, George." When he pulled the trigger, the gun fired, and the buckshot struck my grandpa's right arm. The injury was so severe that the only option was amputation.

Grandpa Chapman and me, 1955

This story haunted my dad through the years, but he never spoke of it. It remained untold, even when I asked about going hunting and mentioned that I would be using a borrowed shotgun. Instead, when the question was posed again, Dad just looked at me for what seemed like forever. With a thoughtful expression, he looked down at his plate and said, "Sure."

Not knowing at that moment how disturbing the images were that had likely passed through Dad's mind when I brought up the invitation, I didn't understand what an emotional stretch it was for him to agree to it. Actually, even though I eventually heard the gruesome story about the cause of Grandpa's disability, to this day I still don't know exactly why Dad gave me the go-ahead that day. Perhaps he felt that it would be beneficial for me as a young teen to experience some adventure in the woods. Maybe he thought being with Kenneth would be better than always hanging out with a band of energetic, mischievous neighborhood boys. Or perhaps he considered Kenneth so trustworthy that he would be a good influence on me spiritually and keep me safe.

I prefer to think that it was for all these reasons that my dad said yes. Whatever the reason was, Dad had no clue that his single word of permission would birth in me a passion that would consume me for the rest of my life. As far as I was concerned at the time, I was just going for an adventure and being nice to a church family member.

I called Mr. Bledsoe that afternoon and told him I would be joining him the next Saturday morning if it was still okay. He sounded very pleased and upbeat as he suggested that I come to his house on Friday after school and stay overnight so my folks wouldn't have to get up before daylight to make the drive. He also said the extra time would give him a chance to outfit me in some proper hunting attire as well as show me some things about handling a gun. I remember hanging up and wondering why he sounded so excited.

Friday came. That evening after supper, Dad drove me to the Bledsoes' house. Dad, Kenneth, and his wife, Evelyn, talked a little while, and then Dad headed home. Before he left, he hugged me and rubbed the back of my head the way he always did. It was his usual show of affection. Looking back now, I'm quite sure it was more than that. No doubt there was a silent, serious prayer said with his gentle, parting touch.

After Dad left, it was time to try on some camouflaged clothes. Mr. Bledsoe's collection didn't include the fancy, modern patterns we wear today. Instead, his gear closet was filled with Army-type camo—the kind he wore when he served our nation in the Korean War. Once again, I was oblivious to any significance. I had no idea of the value and meaning in the clothing. To me, it would simply be what I'd wear for fun.

I was almost as tall as Mr. Bledsoe, but because of my thin, Barney Fife waistline, I had to tighten his belt a few extra inches to keep the pants up. The distance between my chest and the buttons on the coat was at least half a foot. An onlooker would have thought I either had clothes that were way too big or I should be congratulated for having lost a hundred pounds.

Next came Mr. Bledsoe's tutorial about the gun I would use in the morning. It was an over/under type of gun with the .22 rifle topping the 20-gauge shotgun. I would be using the 20-gauge. A lever behind the hammer broke the gun open. Aiming was done using open sights.

With an expended shotgun shell, Mr. Bledsoe showed me how to open the gun, slide a shell into the chamber, snap it closed, and take aim. Much like the gun safety teachers of today would do, he had some things to cover regarding the proper handling of the piece. He spoke sternly.

"The most important things to remember when using a gun is to keep your finger off the trigger until you're ready to fire. Always look beyond the target to make sure you don't see anything that resembles a human or anything else you don't want to shoot. If you have even the slightest question about a target, *don't* take the shot. Once you decide that it's okay to shoot, firmly pull the hammer back until you hear it click into place, put the butt of the stock snugly against your shoulder, line up the front sight with the rear sight, and slowly pull the trigger. Let the gun surprise you when it fires." Then he smiled and added, "This gun will kick a little, but if you're shooting at a squirrel, you won't feel it."

Mr. Bledsoe had me practice loading and unloading the gun. I opened it with the breakdown lever, slid the empty shell into the chamber, snapped it closed just like he showed me, and raised the gun to my shoulder. He nodded his head and, with a look of satisfaction said, "Yep, that's the way you do it. It seems to come natural to you." It must have been both a relief and a confidence-builder for him to see me follow his instructions so well. After all, he was taking a health risk by taking a novice like me hunting.

Though dry-firing a gun wasn't something he favored, Mr. Bledsoe had me pull the hammer back and pull the trigger. It was sobering and a little scary to go through the motions of a shot. I felt different, as if I were being trusted with danger.

After addressing a few more items, such as how to safely carry a gun when walking behind him through the woods and why I should never bring a loaded gun into a house, Mr. Bledsoe stood up and said, "It's time to get some sleep, Steve. Five o'clock is going to come fast. Evelyn will show you the girls' room where you'll be. Ginny and Linda are at a friend's house tonight, so you won't be kept awake by their shenanigans. I'll see you in the a.m."

By the time my head hit the pillow at the Bledsoe residence, I was a tired youngster. A full day at school, a full belly, and an evening filled with lots to remember had me ready for a long snooze. While it didn't take but a minute or two for me to drift off, I could not have known that it would be the last night in my life that I would go to sleep that easy before going hunting the next morning. The next day, a dream would be born in my soul.

Kenneth Bledsoe, hunter extraordinaire and mentor

2

I Awoke to Dream

Five o'clock came on that unforgettable Saturday morning in October. I was sleeping soundly when I thought I heard the faint sound of a man's voice. And something was shaking my shoulder. It took sustained effort for Kenneth to finally break through the wall of my slumber. As my eyes fluttered open, I was confused by the fact that when I went to sleep it was dark and it was still dark when I woke up.

"Steve, it's time to go huntin'. Gotta get up and get ready." I'm not sure how many times Mr. Bledsoe had said those words. I was still a little groggy and thought about protesting the wake-up call, but something got my attention that changed my mind. It wasn't the planned day of hunting or the chance to carry a real shotgun to the woods that had me on full alert. I didn't yet know to be excited by that prospect. Instead, it was an incredibly inviting aroma.

Wafting from Mrs. Bledsoe's kitchen was the intensely appetizing smell of bacon, eggs, and freshly baked biscuits. To a perpetually ravenous teenager whose three-hour feeding schedule had been interrupted by more than six hours of sleep, my nose said, "Get up!" I bounded out of bed, pulling on my pants and shirt before heading to the table.

After I ate enough to fill two adult men, Mr. Bledsoe directed me to their utility room. As I put on the clothes we'd chosen the night before, he said, "When you're ready, meet me outside in the carport."

When I stepped outside, the air was crisp and chilly. I was glad to have on the extra cotton. Kenneth stood in the center of the concrete slab that served as the foundation for his open-air carport. Right above his head was a single, sixty-watt exposed light bulb. I knew that three sides of the carport were open but I couldn't see anything beyond them other than black walls of darkness. It was eerie to think about voluntarily walking out into unlit nothingness. Then again, I felt a twinge of eagerness to find out what it was like.

Mr. Bledsoe...Kenneth...handed me the opened gun, and I draped it across my arm like he'd shown me the night before. He said, "Put your other hand out like this." He demonstrated his instructions by holding his hand out, palm up. I followed his direction and presented my open hand. He reached into his coat pocket and pulled out a half-dozen yellow 20-gauge shotgun shells. He carefully placed them in my palm.

Unlike the light, empty shell we'd used the night before when I learned how to load and unload the gun, the six shells I held in my hand were heavy. My excitement rose even as I realized that what I had in my hand was more than ammunition. I held a heap of powerful projectiles designed to cause something to hurt, bleed, and likely die.

As Kenneth curled my fingertips up so the shells wouldn't fall, he said, "Put those in your coat pocket, and let's go huntin'."

I carefully dropped the shells into the right pocket of my coat and fell in behind my camo-clad host as he turned and walked into the pitch black. Doing exactly as I was told, I stayed within a couple of steps of Kenneth as he walked across his yard, down a short embankment, and onto the pavement of the highway. We quickly crossed the road, stepped into the grassy shoulder, went down another bank, and then entered the woods. At this point, Kenneth stopped. Without looking back at me, he removed a small flashlight from his pocket.

I was relieved. As he continued on, I followed closely, all the while watching the ground at Kenneth's feet that was illuminated by the round, white beam of light. I made sure I stepped in Kenneth's steps. I figured if he felt secure about the ground that was under him, I could feel the same.

Under my rubber boots, I could feel when we started downhill. The walking was easy. We had gone probably 300 yards when Kenneth stopped again. He shined the flashlight on the three strands of barbed wire in front of us. "We need to step over these wires. I'll hold your gun as you do." What he said next still echoes in my mind every time I encounter a fence when hunting.

"Steve, don't ever cross a fence with a gun in your hands. People have been known to die that way." Then he held out his hand to take my gun and proceeded to show me how to safely cross a fence when a gun is in the mix. He leaned the barrel away from us against a post and then crossed a few feet away. From the other side, he pulled the gun through the wires with the barrel pointing away from him. Lesson taught, lesson learned.

We continued through the woods and stopped at a tree with a very thick trunk. I learned later it was a white oak that had probably been standing there since the early 1930s. With his boot-clad foot, Kenneth scraped away the leaves down to the raw earth in a three-foot circle next to the tree. He said softly, "Have a seat."

I sat down on the ground and leaned my back against the oak. The smell of raw earth permeated my senses. After all these years, it's that smell more than any other that triggers a lifetime of hunting memories and a longing to go back to the woods. I've told folks that if I'm ever in a coma, just wave a handful of raw earth under my nose and I'll wake up.

As I sat in the circle of exposed dirt, Kenneth squatted next to me and gave me some instructions that were brief but sounded very important.

"Be on the lookout for squirrels now. I think you're familiar enough with the gun to know how to use it. Again, it'll kick when you fire it, but you won't feel a thing if a squirrel is in your sights. I'm gonna leave you here and go around the hill. Whatever you do, don't go anywhere. I don't want to lose you on this hill. I'll be back in a while to get you."

"Yes, sir."

"Enjoy the morning. Be safe. I'll be back."

With that Kenneth stood up, and within a couple of seconds he disappeared behind what seemed to be a black curtain. All that was left of him was the sound of his footsteps in the crunchy leaves. As the sound faded to quiet, I realized just how alone I was. At that moment, things got emotionally intense. I'd never been by myself in such deep darkness. What was worse, as my eyes adjusted to the environment, the barely visible shapes of things around me looked like tall monsters with their arms up ready to pounce. I felt anxiety rising, which made me second-guess my decision to agree to the hunt.

As though Kenneth knew how much darkness I could endure alone, he had timed my wait perfectly. A few minutes after he left me, light came to the oak tree. The sky slowly started turning gray-blue, and very soon the top edge of the sun peeked over the horizon. Gradually the woods filled with light. The figures that looked like monsters became ivy-covered trees. I felt safe again.

Once my nerves settled, I realized there were sounds I hadn't noticed before. Birds were chirping overhead, in the distance crows were cawing and somewhere way down in the hollow I heard roosters crowing. Nearby, I could hear something scampering across the leafy floor of the woods. I found out later they were chipmunks that had awakened and were starting their daily search for breakfast.

I was surprised by an overwhelming sense of joy that welled up inside me. I realized I was in love with where I was, what I was hearing, and what I was doing. It was as though I had lived in a house for thirteen years and then discovered a room I didn't know was there. The place was filled with a symphony of beautiful sounds and an array of brilliant shades of orange, yellow, and red against a backdrop of various brown hues. In a matter of minutes, I went from being just another young teen on the streets to becoming a bona fide young man of the woods. I was suddenly a hunter—and I knew it deep in my heart.

As I sat quietly with my senses immersed in the colorful yet quiet environment of the West Virginia woods, I had no idea what was about to happen. Suddenly, with no warning from behind me, I felt a couple of firm taps on my shoulder. My entire body stiffened. I thought, *Should I turn around and see what's about to eat me?*

When I finally found the courage to turn my head, I couldn't believe what—actually who—I saw. It was Kenneth. With full voice I said, "How did you do that? How did you sneak up on me without me hearing you?"

Kenneth put his finger over his lips in the universal quiet sign and squatted again to talk. "See anything, Steve?"

"No, sir. Well, I didn't see any squirrels to shoot at."

Kenneth didn't seem surprised, nor did he appear disappointed. No doubt the excited look on my face as I told him about what I *had* seen and heard during the morning let him know that I had enjoyed the experience. Then he said something I didn't want to hear, and I could see that he dreaded to say it.

"The hunt is over, Steve."

The saddest words a golfer can hear are "It's still your turn." A motorcyclist never wants someone to tell him, "That's gonna hurt." And the words a hunter dreads the most are, "The hunt is over." Reluctantly, I got up and followed Kenneth back up the hill toward his house.

I didn't fire a shot that morning for two good reasons. One, I didn't know I was supposed to sit as still as possible. I had shifted around, used the "bath tree" a couple of times, and occasionally raised the gun to practice the shooting routine. Every critter in the county knew I was there. Second, I had snuck in a few snacks in my coat, and the candy wrappers that were strewn around me didn't help my cause. Though my game bag was empty, I left the woods that day with a heart full of "want to." It's still there. From that day forward, I woke up and started dreaming of a future filled with hunting.

Singing in church with Dad and
Kenneth and Evelyn Bledsoe

Kenneth with a Canadian caribou

3

Feeding the Dream

I sat in church the next morning looking at my dad as he preached, but I didn't hear a word he said. In my mind I kept hitting the replay button on the recorded memories of my time in the timber on the hillside below Kenneth's house. I wondered if Kenneth would come to me after church like he did the Sunday before and invite me to go with him again.

Monday morning at school was no different when it came to struggling to concentrate on anything but hunting. Actually, the whole week was a blur. I couldn't stop thinking about how good it felt to be sitting on the ground under that huge oak tree with a shotgun on my lap. I could still smell the raw earth under me and hear the distant sound of crows cawing. It was a glorious distraction.

I tried hard to not let academics interfere with my recall of the hunt, but the pesky tests I had to study for and the stacks of homework the teachers gave made it really hard to do. I wondered how long it would be before I'd get to feed the dream to hunt again. Until then, what could I do to learn more about it? Then I discovered something that was, in my estimation, providential. It happened one morning at our local pharmacy.

In the back corner of the store was a soda fountain I visited whenever I came into some money. The fare included sandwiches, hot dogs, and a few other lunch items. But there was another reason I went. I craved their Cherry Coke and cream-filled donuts.

As I sat at the counter happily ingesting at least forty grams of sugar into my youthful bloodstream, I turned on the swiveling stool and stopped for a moment facing the shelves across the aisle. They were lined with magazines. I'd never paid a whole lot of attention to them, but for some reason I scanned the array of covers. There were pictures of fancily dressed women modeling the latest fashions, cooked dishes of food, famous people's pictures, and some late-model cars. Suddenly, my eyes caught sight of the cover of a magazine that made me stop chewing my mouthful of donut. It had a painting of a whitetail buck looking my way and seeming to say, "Come and find me—if you can!" Above the deer in large, bold, black letters outlined in red were the words *Fur-Fish-Game.*

Fur-Fish-Game…still feeding the dream

My heart leaped with excitement that such a magazine even existed. I put my donut down on the counter, walked across the aisle, and took a copy off the shelf. With sticky sugar still on my fingers, I leafed through pages of photos of squirrel, deer, mountains, and streams. I knew instantly that I had to have a copy! I dug through my pockets for the twenty-five cents required to buy it. It was the first of many issues of *Fur-Fish-Game* that I would spend my hard-begged money on. I considered them to be more than entertainment. For a young hunter who was eager to learn everything about the fair chase, they would become my monthly textbook.

Some of the covers featured photos of hunters in moments they'd lived in the wild, but it was the covers with paintings that I liked best. There seemed to be more mystery in the watercolor and oil depictions of outdoor scenes. It was as though I were dreamily looking ahead at things that were going to happen, the kind of things I had yet to experience. Seeing a painting of a deer jumping over a fence, a squirrel in flight from one tree limb to another, a fox walking through a snowy field, or a beagle chasing a cottontail seemed more futuristic when depicted in a painting. Each cover of that type served to spoon-feed a ravenous appetite to actually experience the moments in the artful renderings.

The stories inside were written by outdoorsmen of every type. They knew how to get my hunting juices flowing. My imagination ran wild as I read the well-written stories. The authors succeeded in filling my plate with dream food when they wrote about things like stalking a big buck and having to crawl on hands and knees over a hundred yards to close the deal. Their accounts of calling ducks to within shotgun distance, standing in fields as their well-trained beagles brought rabbits in a big circle back to where they stood, and how peaceful they felt while sitting on a mountaintop glassing for mountain goats generated a wide range of welcomed emotions in my soul.

I was so attracted to hunting that I even read every advertisement! The small ads featured countless items that were available by mail order, and each one came with a promise to make me a more successful hunter. Pictures of everything from bottled fox urine deer hunters could use for masking their scents to the latest and greatest predator calls were there to drool over.

Each issue I could get my hands on was soon dog-eared from repeatedly turning the pages. I eventually found other hunting magazines—*Outdoor Life*, *Field & Stream*, and *Sports Afield*. The pages of these monthlies were also well stocked with pictures and stories that fed my growing passion for hunting. Each one had paper that was a little heavier and a bit glossier, the page count was greater, and the layout seemed a little slicker. But as nice and informative as they were, the simplicity and down-home feeling of *Fur-Fish-Game* kept me coming back.

My intake of information about hunting was so constant that within a matter of a few short months after my first morning in the woods, I had become a "huntaholic." I couldn't drink in enough about the subject to satisfy my thirst. And as if I needed more, another media source came along in the mid-1960s that fed my hunting craving. It was a TV show called *The American Sportsman*, hosted by well-known sportscaster Curt Gowdy.

I couldn't wait until Sunday afternoons to hear the familiar musical theme announce the start of the show. The images on the screen of hunters carrying their guns and bows into the woods and fields of America were impressed on my mind like a hot brand on a cow's hip. I would go to bed Sunday nights dreading the sleep that would come and end my dream of doing what I saw the hunters doing on TV that afternoon.

As I headed toward my senior year in high school, the combination of getting to hunt small game from time to time with Kenneth, the inspiring magazine covers, the action photos and countless informative articles, and the adventure-packed TV shows did plenty to feed the hunting dream. I even joined the Rod and Gun Club at school, where I could swap stories with other guys who were as obsessed with hunting as I was.

Of the hunters I met in the halls of Point Pleasant High School, I was surprised and happy to find out that one of them lived just down the road from the Bledsoe family. His very name bore the mark of a hunter: Greg Bonecutter. He too was a dream-feeder for me not only through our conversations but also with occasional invitations to join him on his dad's farm to chase squirrels, rabbits, crows, and anything else we could legally hunt. One of my trips to his hunting ground involved a Friday afternoon bus ride after school. (If I did today what I did that day in 1964, I would end up in jail.)

Knowing that after school I would board the bus with Greg that carried students out Sand Hill Road, I went home for lunch on that Friday. My dad, who had become more confident over time with my having a shotgun, had bought a Harrington-Richardson (H&R) single-shot 20-gauge for me that broke down into three pieces. I put the butt stock and forend in a large paper grocery bag and slid the barrel down my pants and hung it on my waist belt.

I went back to school and walked the halls with a limp. I looked like the gimpy character Chester on the old TV show *Gunsmoke*. No one asked about my lame leg. Even the bus driver didn't seem to notice it when I boarded her bus. Amazingly, I made it all the way to Greg's house without incident. I can't imagine what a ruckus I'd create if I tried that stunt now!

While Greg and I wandered the hills together as hunters, we talked about the outdoor magazine stories, all the amazing photos, and the one TV hunting show we both lived to see on Sunday afternoons. Our imaginations ran wild as we wondered what it would be like to venture into the depths of mountainous territories like Montana and Idaho, where animals like the majestic elk and bighorn sheep lived.

One day, three words came together that conjured up my idea of the greatest adventure I would ever know. Fulfilling this quest would be like summiting the Mount Everest of hunts. My dream was to chase the *Alaska brown bear*!

Just saying the name Alaska made the gears of my brain grind and smoke as I tried to imagine how far away it was from Mason County, West Virginia. My questions were many. *What does 3000 miles away from home feel like? How long would it take to get there, and how would I get there? Just how cold is it in Alaska? Could I hunt there by myself?*

The hair on the back of my young neck stood when the image of a giant, monstrous, big-toothed, powerful, thick-furred, scared-of-nothing-on-the-planet brown bear passed through my head—and this was just from what I saw in photos. How could I possibly be brave enough to face one in the wild? Being naive enough to ignore the reality of the danger and think only of the adventure, I wanted to find out. The odds against me seemed to say "Dream on," and so I did.

Greg and me today—old friends of the woods

4

Committed to the Cause

I was introduced to hunting when I was about two months into my second year of junior high. As the school year progressed, my interest in being a hunter intensified so much that when small game season closed after Christmas I basically went into mourning. Waiting through the rest of winter, springtime, and then summer vacation for the following fall season to come wasn't easy to say the least. But it wasn't as tough as what I faced when the new school year finally did arrive. I had to decide if I would play basketball or focus on being a hunter. Or could I do both?

My skill level on the court was only fair, but I enjoyed the game and thought I might be good enough to make the team if I entered tryouts. I knew it would be a juggling act between playing ball and hunting, but I decided to see if I could make it work. The games were played during the week, which would leave the weekends to head to the woods. When tryouts came, I put my best sneaker forward. The day finally arrived when the coach would pick his players.

I won't forget the afternoon when the coach blew his whistle and called all the wannabes to the foul circle, where he would announce the names of those who had made the squad. When I heard him say those magical words, "Chapman, go get your Converses," I couldn't believe my ears. I was on the team!

Everything was going fine until opening day of squirrel season. In order to be in the woods with Kenneth on Saturday morning, I went to the Bledsoe house on Friday to spend the night. I intentionally forgot that our coach had called for a practice on Saturday to prepare for a very important game the next week. I had a great Saturday in the woods and gave no thought to the trouble that awaited me when the weekend was over.

Monday afternoon, practice time came. I got dressed in the locker room and headed to the gym floor. The coach came over and asked, "Where were you Saturday, Chapman?"

"Uh…well, sir…I went huntin'."

Coach was unsympathetic to the fact that the first day of season in West Virginia was akin to a national holiday. Because he didn't accommodate the tradition, I fell victim to grace withheld. His response to my admission that I skipped Saturday practice proved it.

"Okay. Drop and give me fifty."

I had heard those dreaded words spoken before, but not to me. I knew I was in trouble and sighed deeply as I faced the shiny hardwood floor in the push-up position. I started counting and struggled with my skinny arms to obey the coach's command. The pain in my biceps quickly intensified as I repeatedly fought to push my body upward… and so did the voice in my head that asked, *Would I rather hunt or play basketball?*

I argued with myself through another seven or eight pushups, and suddenly there was a winner in the argument. My dream of being the next Jerry West was overridden by my dream of being the next Fred Bear. (Young'uns might have to ask your grandparents who these two legends were.)

Before I could talk myself out of making a rash decision, I stood up, put my shoulders back, raised my chin, and walked over to the coach. He turned around, put his clipboard up under his left arm, placed his right hand on his hip, and asked with a tone of doubt, "You've done fifty already?"

"Well, sir, no." I reached down and took off my Converses before I finished. "I'm sorry, but I think I'd rather hunt than play basketball. You can have these back."

Coach just looked at me and didn't protest as he took the barely used shoes.

"If that's what you prefer, Chapman, you're welcome to go."

I've never actually known if his lack of resistance to the idea of losing a player was based on my second-string level of round-ball skill or his appreciation of a young man who obviously and confidently knew what he wanted and was willing to sacrifice for it. More than likely, it was the former.

I walked out of the gymnasium with my eyes fixed on being a man of the deep woods instead a man of the hardwood. Except for the decisions I made to be a Christ follower and choose to marry Annie, no other choice has impacted my life more than committing that day to be a dedicated hunter.

For the next fifty years, I followed the trail of adventure through West Virginia, Ohio, Tennessee, Kentucky, Arizona, Indiana, New Jersey, Mississippi, Alabama, Arkansas, Missouri, New York, Wyoming, Colorado, Montana, South Dakota, North Dakota, Kansas, Wisconsin, and even Germany.

In time, my "where I've hunted" list would grow to include some awesome places that yielded incredible memories, each one as valuable as gold to me. But as lengthy as the list was, when late 2013 came, there was one dream name yet to be added—Alaska. The annual seasons kept passing, and I kept dreaming. I was heading toward my midsixties, and it looked as though that dream would never come true.

As I had done in the past when it came to dealing with unfulfilled wishes, I decided the best thing to do was to put the longing in the hands of God. I did it because I believe He knows what's best for me. I didn't doubt He knew that one of my wishes was to someday walk on Alaskan soil as a hunter. Who better to trust than Him? It was the right thing to do.

Sometimes when we release our tightly held longings and give them to God, He rewards our surrender by granting the desires of our heart—and occasionally in the most unexpected way. Maybe He does this so we'll have no doubt whom to thank, or maybe His purpose is to help us learn to put more trust in Him. Either way, I was certainly grateful for what happened in early 2014. I won't forget opening my email on my phone and finding a message that I had to read twice to make sure I was reading it right. It was a simple question asked by a friend.

"Steve, would you be interested in joining me in the spring of 2015 on a trip to hunt for brown bear in Alaska?"

Yee haw and hallelujah!

Awesome Alaska

5

The Unbelievable Email

I was almost beside myself as I processed the invitation to join my friend on a hunt in Alaska. I stood in my office and spoke to my phone. "Unbelievable! Alaska? Are you kidding? Pinch me!"

Annie heard my one-sided conversation and asked if something was wrong. I read the message to her so she would know what had me all keyed up. I looked closely again at the address line to make sure it was meant for me. It was!

I asked my beloved what she thought about the message. She smiled big and said, "Wow! How could you possibly refuse?" I love that woman!

My fingers shook so much I could hardly type my response. "Definitely interested. When is it happening?"

I knew my friend was a busy man, so I was pleasantly surprised that it took only a few minutes to get a reply with the month and dates. When I saw the message icon pop up in my email, I nervously opened it.

"May 10–20, 2015. Let me know if you can do it so I can secure it."

My stomach churned as I checked Annie's and my itinerary to see if we had concert or seminar dates scheduled in May that would prevent my going. We didn't! I immediately shot an email to our booking office to double-check if anything was pending for those dates. The two-hour wait for a response was painful, but our agent finally sent a message saying the dates were open.

I quickly replied, "Hold the dates for me, plus two on each side… there's a chance that a bear hunt in Alaska is in the making!"

Our scheduler instantly emailed, "So should I go ahead and cancel all concerts after May 21?"

I stared at his words and half-grinned at the implication in his question about the possible health risks that come with being in bear country. I was too excited about the invitation to give them serious consideration.

I replied, "No need. I expect to make it back 'cause I've heard bears don't like the taste of starving musicians."

Within a minute I saw his reply. "You're mean!"

Later that evening I typed an email to the man who had extended the hunting invitation. When I hit Send, I prayed, *Lord, whether or not this hunt actually happens, I ask that You will pour upon this kind saint the very best of Your blessings if for no other reason than the joy his invitation has heaped upon me.*

It was four days, eight hours, twelve minutes, and twenty-nine seconds before I heard back. I had assumed that the details of planning such a trip were quite involved and required some time, but it didn't help quiet the anxiety I felt about whether or not it was going to happen. Finally, another message from him appeared on my phone. It was layered with reasons to feel elated.

"It's a go, and it's on me. And is there someone you want to bring with you to video the hunt and take pictures for us?"

"Whoa!" I said aloud and then said it again. "Whoa!" There were three tiers of incredibleness to mentally and emotionally process. One, I was going to Alaska! Two, the cost was covered! Three, I could bring a friend! My knees, elbows, hips, and brain buckled. All I could do was repeat, "Whoa!"

No doubt you're wondering who stuffed my game bag with such an awesome invitation and what his phone number is. Well, I will honor his wish for anonymity, but in the halls of heaven the secret is out, and as far as I'm concerned there is still talk on the golden streets about what a monumentally good deed was done down here on earth for one of God's children.

Stunned by the confirmation of the hunt, the covered cost, and the opportunity ahead to totally surprise and bless a friend, I was lost for the right words to sufficiently express my thanks for such kindness. I knew from the onset that I would never, ever be able to fully repay the man. The truth was, I knew I could never afford such a trip. Without this gift, I wouldn't be going. It was a blessing beyond belief.

I would eventually learn that all my friend wanted in return was the pleasure of knowing I would totally immerse myself in the thrill that the experience would yield and that I would love tending to every little detail required to get ready for it. And that's exactly what I did.

6

That's What Friends Are For

After it was settled that I would be going to Alaska to hunt, the next step was to decide whom to call and invite to go with me. I wondered, *Who can I bless in the way that my friend has blessed me?*

I first thought of my son, Nathan. He's an incredibly gifted photographer and enjoys hunting. However, I thought of four very important reasons why he might not be able to participate. His wife and two very young children who needed every minute he could spare were three of the reasons. The fourth was his reputation for being a respected, Grammy-winning, sought-after music producer and songwriter in Nashville. These roles kept him busier than a wing on a hummingbird. For him to give up nearly two weeks away from his family and job would not work well for him at that time in his life.

My son-in-law, Emmitt, also loved hunting and had a good camera, but he faced the same challenges as Nathan. His attention to Heidi and their three lovely little girls and his job as CFO of a huge national company would make it difficult for him to take an extended time away.

So whom would I invite? I needed someone whose kids were raised, whose job was flexible, and whose skills with both a still camera and recording equipment were advanced. Also, he had to understand that hunting can require being motionless in one moment and on the run the next. I knew exactly who to call.

My heart was pounding as I touched the initials LW on my phone's Favorites page. I composed myself as Lindsey Williams's phone started ringing. Because it was the mobile number he used for business, he answered as he always did: "This is Lindsey."

"What's up, dude?" I tried not to give away my excitement.

"Just makin' some music over here."

Lindsey's work in the field of broadcast music kept him hopping in his home studio making songs that a lot of people have heard but don't know who is behind them. His creations have been used as promo music for *Late Night with David Letterman*, NBC's *Today Show*, and a host of national TV ads for companies such as Subaru…just to name a few.

My musical connection to Lindsey came about when he agreed to produce a couple of CDs for Annie and me as well as our company's best recording so far, *Hymns from God's Great Cathedral*. It features the soothing voice of our daughter, Heidi, singing ten pre-1900 hymns. And being the outdoors people we are, we included the calming sounds of nature in the background.

Lindsey and me on a two-bird day

While Lindsey and I had a mutual interest in music, there was something else we shared that prompted me to call him about going to Alaska. We have spent many days together chasing deer, turkey, rabbits, ducks, and elk. For this reason, he's very aware of what is required of a hunter. He also knows about working together in the wild as a team. On more than one occasion we've accomplished near impossibilities. One is a feat in turkey hunting known as a double—sitting side by side and taking two mature, extremely keen-eyed gobblers. The second is helping each other get deer with a one-man drive. It's rarely successful, but more than once it has yielded meat for our freezers.

Along with his music and hunting skills, Lindsey is a student of the camera. It's hard to tell how many screen savers on my desktop have featured his photography. Plus, he'd worked with a videographer in the past, and I knew his understanding of filming went beyond the basics.

Feeling completely confident that Lindsey was the buddy to invite, I continued our phone conversation.

"Hey man, I've been in touch with a gentleman who has invited me to join him on a brown bear hunt in Alaska next spring."

Graciously, Lindsey congratulated me. "Wow! That's awesome. Tell me you're gonna do it!"

"It looks like I'm in, but I have some news for you. The fellow who invited me wants to know if there's someone I want to bring along for taking pictures and capturing the hunt on video. Would you be up for that?"

If we'd been using Facetime, I know I would have seen my friend's eyes widen when he heard my question. I could hear it in his voice when he answered.

"Well...uh...*yes*! You know I'd be up for that! But, dude, how many millions of dollars will it cost?"

I couldn't get the words out of my mouth fast enough. "Just the cost of the ticket to get to Sitka and whatever else you'd need in order to spend ten days in the great state of Alaska!"

"What? Are you kidding?"

I could tell Lindsey was seriously struggling to believe what I said. I didn't want him to think I was making a joke (because he might drive over to my house and do some of that "dance, pilgrim" gunfire at my feet), so I quickly confirmed the invitation as fact.

"I'm as serious as the heart attack you had a few years ago. There's room for four on the hunt—our host, a hunter he's bringing from his hometown, myself as a hunter, and an added participant to carry the cameras."

Lindsey could hardly get the words out. "Well, what month next spring and how many days?"

"The trip will span May 10–20 of 2015. I've blocked two days on each side of those dates for travel. Check with Susan, promise her the moon and two planets if you have to, clear your calendar, and tell me you can do it."

"I'll do my best. Thanks, man!"

I touched the red End Call button on my phone and tried to imagine the amount of joy that was coursing through my friend's veins at that moment. I could almost see him walking out of his studio and heading downstairs to tell his wife about my call. I had a feeling he was quickly thinking about how to say it in a way that would put most of the emphasis on the chance to travel to an awesome place he'd never been without bringing too much attention to the massive meat-eating creatures that lived there.

I don't know what he said, what he promised, or if he was on his knees when he brought up the idea, but it worked. I got his call later that day.

"Susan's good with it. I have airline miles to use to get to Sitka and back. I'm in!"

"That's good news, man. Now there's just one thing I've gotta do to get ready to hunt the mighty brown bear with you."

"What's that?"

"I gotta start running every day."

"Why?" Lindsey started hunting later in life, and he'd not been around hunters long enough to have heard the punch line I couldn't wait to deliver. I was delighted that he would hear it from me first.

"So I can outrun you, dude! They say a brown bear can run thirty miles per hour!"

Lindsey's voice went lower and more serious sounding as he said, "Well, that's a tidbit I won't be sharing with Susan."

Our supportive wives, Annie and Susan

7

Preparing—Step 1

Don't Worry

The absolutely glorious shock that came with the invitation to hunt brown bear in Alaska didn't fade. The thought of what an awesome trip was in my future repeatedly rolled over me like big, warm waves on a southern ocean beach. I welcomed each one. But there was another thought, actually a question, that would come from time to time that I didn't welcome. *What if something happens that prevents me from going?*

I thought of a few plan-halting possibilities. An unfortunate and unexpected health issue could pop up in a man of my age. A family member could get sick or injured. Our house could burn to the ground or be wiped away in a tornado. These imagined circumstances and more taunted me.

As the list of potential adventure-destroying ideas grew, I recalled what I heard someone say years ago: "There is no grace for borrowed sorrow." I was guilty of borrowing plenty of it. I finally came to grips with the fact that the first step in preparing to go to Alaska was to stop planting doubt and fear in my own head. Instead, I had to deliberately choose to believe that God orders my steps. If He wanted me to go hunting in Alaska, nothing could stop it. And if it wasn't meant to be, He would have a good reason to prevent it. I knew that holding the adventure with an "open hand" attitude was best, but it wasn't all that easy to do.

With some concerted effort to control my thoughts, I managed to release most of the worrisome, fantasized reasons for not being in Alaska come next spring. However, there was one that was very real and worthy of serious consideration. It was my dad's health. He was nearing 90 years of age and struggling with early stage congestive heart failure. There was no way to predict what his condition would be by the time the following spring arrived. The thought of being 3000 miles away for a long string of days with a very limited ability, if any, to connect with him made me feel uneasy.

Once again I had to let go of the worry, stop borrowing sorrow, and intentionally leave the future in God's capable hands. In the meantime, there were a lot of other things to do to get ready to head northwest.

Dad and me

8

Preparing—Step 2

The List

Deciding to hold the trip to Alaska with an open hand eliminated the nagging worry that it wouldn't happen and made it a lot more enjoyable to move to step two of preparation. It was time to make a list of what I needed to have, what I needed to do, and what I needed to get before the day of departure.

In order to intelligently compile the list, the first thing I did was email the gentleman who extended the invitation. Because he'd been on this kind of hunt several times, I called on his experience. Here is what he sent me. Next to each item in brackets is what went through my head when I read the list.

> Steve,
>
> The temperature in Alaska in May can be anywhere from the 30s to 70s, so dress in layers. Make sure your raincoat is large enough to cover your clothes and your coat. It often rains and can be windy as well. [Warning taken!] Here's a list of what you'll need.
>
> - 1 pair of waders [Why waders? Mine leak—gotta get a new pair.]
> - 1 pair of hip boots—optional [Don't have. Optional? Do I need waders and hip boots?]

- 1 pair of boat shoes [Never had a pair; gotta get 'em. What are boat shoes anyway?]
- 1 raincoat [Got it.]
- 1 light rain suit—top and bottom [Got it.]
- 1 rain hat [If he means a wide brim, don't have. Gotta get one.]
- 1 pair of rain gloves—will get in Alaska [That's good 'cause I'm not sure what rain gloves are.]
- 1 rainproof daypack [Is this different from the backpack I carry when I deer hunt?]
- 1-2 hunting pants—jeans are fine [Got 'em.]
- 1-2 hunting shirts [Got 'em.]
- 2 sets long underwear—top and bottom [Got 'em.]
- Regular underwear [Definitely better than irregular underwear.]
- Toiletries—there is a shower on the main boat [I like the sound of that.]
- Socks [I assume if he mentions socks he means something heavy and warm. I'll take the ones that have a pocket for toe warmers—it is Alaska!]
- 1 pair of gloves [Got 'em.]
- 1 regular hat [Got it.]
- Binoculars [Will the little binocs I use here in Tennessee be enough?]
- Camera [Gonna lean on Lindsey for the still camera and buy a video camera for him to use. Surely Annie will understand.]
- 2 boxes of shells in original case and packed in checked luggage [Hmm…wonder what caliber. Can I use my .270 Ruger?]
- 1 hard gun case—must be locked for airlines regs [My

old one is tacky…gotta have a new one. Annie won't mind—I hope.]

- Scope covers [Lost 'em last season, gotta get new set—must really be rainy up there.]

I have reservations in Sitka on May 9 and 10 at the Westmark Hotel. The boat leaves the dock on the morning of May 11. [Gotta remember to tell Annie that I'll be gone one day longer than originally planned—she won't mind—I hope.]

Sitka is a small island town, very beautiful. When you arrive, take a taxi to the hotel.

After I finished looking over the list, I knew I had to get some things. I also needed some clarification on a few items. I sent another message with questions. His responses are in brackets.

Thanks for the list. I appreciate your time in putting it together. I have a few questions as I start to gather the items.

- I assume duck-hunting-type waders are okay. Just curious why we need them. In regard to hip boots being optional, can I bring one or the other? [We'll be using a skiff to get from the main boat to shore where we'll hunt. The shoreline is very rocky, and to keep the skiff from being damaged it needs to be anchored away from the beach. That means we'll be getting out of the skiff and walking through water that's sometimes up to our waist. The waders are necessary to keep you dry. Some hunters like the hip boots instead of waders. The problem with hip boots is when you get out of the skiff, if the water level is higher than the top of the boots they'll fill up, and believe me, the water is painfully cold. For that reason I prefer using waders.]
- What do you mean by "boat shoes?" [Boat shoes are

comfortable shoes to wear on the main boat so you're not walking on the inside decks in your big boots. Speaking of boots, if you get waders with sock feet, you'll need a good pair of boots that work well on slippery rocks.]

- What are rainproof gloves? [They are rubber-coated gloves that a lot of the local fishermen use. They're lined with wool and keep your hands warm and dry. You'll be glad you have them when you're in the skiff! They sell them by the thousands in Sitka. We'll get them there.]
- Is a waterproof daypack different from a regular backpack? [The ride in the skiff can be very wet. If the wind and waves are up, we'll get a lot of spray over the bow. A rainproof daypack is needed to keep your extra clothes, food, gear, and especially your cameras from getting soaked. The water is saltwater, and it can ruin a good camera really quick if it gets soaked. You'll find a dry pack in the camping or marine section at a sporting goods store or online.]
- As for a gun, I have a .270 rifle and use 150-grain bullets. What caliber do you use? [A .270 is a great gun, but it's underpowered for brown bear. The guide won't allow it because it doesn't pack enough punch. I hope you have something bigger.]

I was grateful for the added information and was feeling really good about being able to get everything he noted—until I got to his response about my .270 rifle. When I saw that it wasn't a big enough caliber gun, in my mind I suddenly saw myself standing in a gun shop with my hand shaking as I wrote a large check for a new, big-bore rifle. The guy behind the counter was smiling because the cost of his kid's braces just got covered. I thought, *Just how big a gun do I need?*

I sent another email and asked for a recommendation regarding a caliber to use. His response included a couple of suggested calibers, both of which I'd never had to my shoulder. They were a .458 Winchester Mag, which the guide used, or a .325 Short Mag.

I didn't know anyone who had a gun of either size that I could borrow, so I sat down at my desktop and browsed the Internet to find out what size government loan I'd have to apply for to pay for either one. Most of the guns sold for just under a thousand "bears" (instead of bucks), but it might as well have been in the millions. How could I possibly justify the purchase of a gun like those I saw on the web? Before I could begin rehearsing some sweet gun-buying talk for Annie, I got another email from my friend. I couldn't believe what was in the message.

> Steve, if you don't have a gun bigger than a .270, let me know. I've been thinking about picking up a couple of .325 Short Mags for my grandsons to use when we go after the big stuff. You can use one of them.

I can't fully explain how humbled I felt in that moment. Not only was the man covering the hunt for my friend and me, he was offering to provide the appropriate gun. My heart swelled with gratitude as I processed the incredible gesture. I sat in my chair and shook my head in amazement. I smiled as I had another thought. *I wonder if he got the idea to pick up the power-punching .325s when he saw I only had a big-bear-annoying .270. Did he consider it a matter of self-preservation in case he happened to be next to me when a brownie was nearby?*

I searched for more words than just "thank you" to put in my reply, but I didn't know what else to say. I decided a phone call would be better. I wanted him to hear the gratitude in my voice. During the call, I learned that he was not only getting a pair of .325s but also buying heavy-duty flight cases and shipping a gun to me a few months before the hunt so I could sight it in and get used to it. I hung up the phone knowing that in heaven this man would have double-tiered crowns and an extra layer of gold on the streets he'd be walking on.

9

Preparing—Step 3

And the List Goes On

Thankful to have the rifle issue settled, I turned my focus to the items on the rest of my generous friend's list. The process of finding a good pair of waders, boat shoes, a waterproof daypack, a quality video camera, and everything else I'd need for the hunt wasn't a chore—not in the least. Instead, it was unadulterated, absolute, complete joy! If you're a serious hunter, you understand what I mean. If you're a novice...well, I'll try to explain.

Next to actually being on the ground and engaging in the hunt, making preparations and gathering gear accounts for much of the enjoyment of the outing. When I get ready to hunt deer in Tennessee, for example, I start weeks in advance of opening day with the preparations. I usually begin by inspecting my camo to see if I need to ask Annie to sew any rips that happened in the previous season. Camo that suffered too much damage from briars and barbed-wire fences has to be replaced, which requires a welcome shopping adventure in the aisles of a sporting-goods store.

Once my camo wardrobe is complete, I wash every piece in scent-free soap and hang each one in the sun to dry. Then I half-fill 33-gallon trash bags with dead leaves and add the dry camo so it can "marinate" to cover any additional human scents.

Checking my archery equipment from limb to limb, replacing the string if needed, and replacing dulled broad-head blades and injured arrows are a few more things to cover before bow season starts. For muzzleloader and rifle seasons, I clean the guns, get fresh powder for the smoke pole, fire each type to make sure the scopes are still on target, and more.

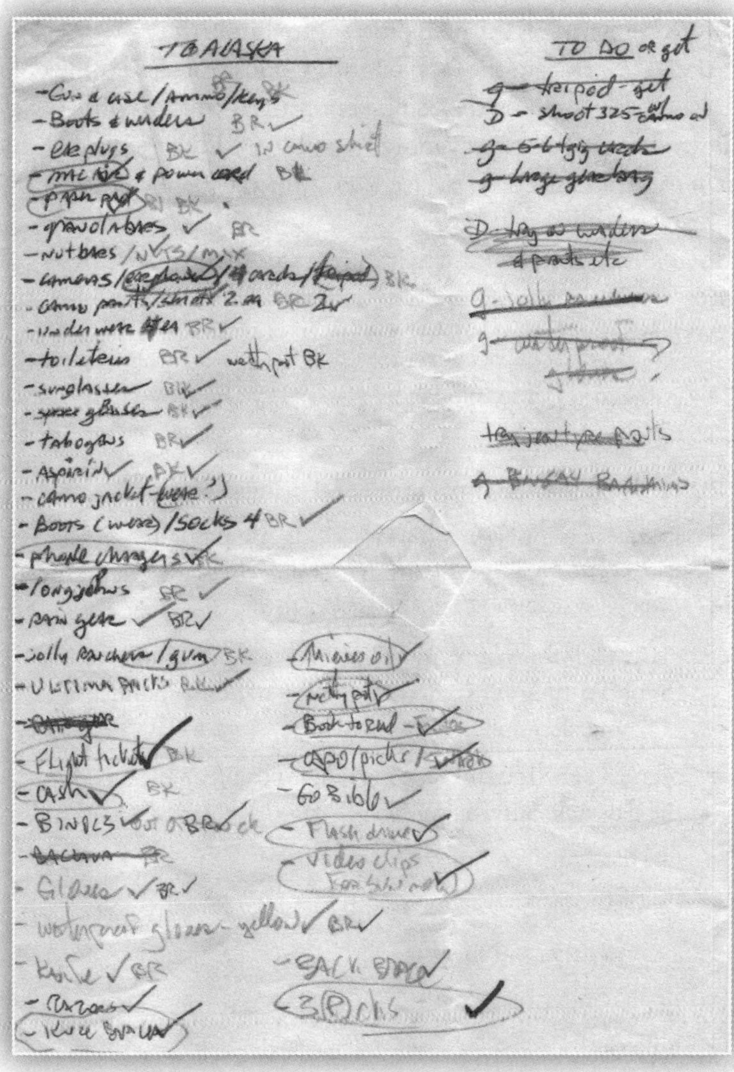

My handwritten Alaska hunt prep list

I never dread these tasks. I approach them with wide-eyed excitement because as I'm doing them, I find myself dreaming about what might happen after giving attention to these details. When I'm freshening and marinating my camo in the dried leaves, I envision a mature buck or keen-eyed doe walking under my tree stand and not knowing I'm in the world. When I'm sighting in my bow or gun, I picture deer walking out into a field or out of a thicket into an opening in the timber. Dreaming makes the prep process pure fun!

After a few trips to the local hunting-goods store and some online purchases, each item on the equipment list was checked off. However, I knew very well there was more I would need for the hunt, which meant the fun wasn't over. In fact, it continued through all the months prior to departure.

Here's my complete list, with explanations in parentheses. The entries aren't categorized and are somewhat disconnected because I wrote them down as I thought of them.

- gun, ammo, case, and keys
- boots and waders
- ear plugs (for the airplane ride and firing the gun)
- iMac Air and power cord (for writing my thoughts—and I had a book manuscript due in October that I'd work on if time permitted)
- paper pad (for writing more lists and making a song set list for performing at a local church in Sitka on the Sunday morning after our arrival)
- granola bars (It didn't take me long to think about food for the daypack. Survival was on my mind.)
- nut bars, nuts, and mix
- cameras, earphones, four 64GB memory cards, tripod
- 2 camo pants and shirts
- 4 pairs underwear
- toiletries

- neti pot (to protect against colds—a singer's burden to carry)
- sunglasses
- spare reading glasses
- toboggan hat
- aspirin
- camo jacket
- boots and four pairs of socks (including the pair with toe warmer pockets)
- phone and chargers
- long johns
- rain gear
- Jolly Ranchers and gum (my favorite hard candy—a treat on flights and hunting stands)
- Ultima packs (A sugar-free, powdered electrolyte to add to water. I use it instead of Gatorade.)
- flight tickets
- cash
- binoculars
- balaclava
- gloves
- waterproof gloves (kitchen-type rubber gloves for field dressing a bear—hopefully)
- hunting knife
- razors (for shaving)
- knee brace
- Thieves Essential Oil (I usually carry a small bottle of this blend of essential oils when I travel, especially by air. A drop rubbed under my nostrils is like a small vacation. It can hide the smell of BO, bad breath, and other foul odors people emit.)

- *Prepare!* (former pastor Don Finto's book about getting ready for the end times)
- capo, picks, Snark tuner (for the guitar I would borrow for singing at the church in Sitka)
- Go Bible (MP3 player with the New International Version of the Bible)
- flash drive (for storing text entered in my laptop)
- video clips for Sunday morning (I use video clips during my performances.)
- back brace (After falling out of a tree stand several years ago, any heavy pulling or lifting is best done wearing a back brace. I'd heard that a brown bear can weigh more than 1000 pounds. The brace would be stashed in my daypack.)
- 3 personal checks, 2 business checks (I'm an old timer who still writes a check when I pay for things.)

Next is my "To Do or Get" list.

- tripod (I needed a shorter tripod for the video camera.)
- shoot .325 while wearing camo
- five 64GB memory cards (one in the camera and four spares)
- large gear bag
- try on waders, pants, etc.
- Jolly Ranchers
- waterproof gloves
- Bengay stick on pads for backaches (an essential for a senior citizen)

10

Preparing—Step 4

"Duress Rehearsal"

If Lindsey and I had a dollar for every minute we spent tending to the lists of things to do and get for our journey to Alaska, we could have bought a yacht. Of course, as hunters we were having the time of our lives getting ready to enjoy the time of our lives.

To help my buddy out, I passed along all the "what you'll need" notes and lists from our host. It was late summer, and our departure wasn't until the following May, but we were so pumped about going that by mid-fall everything but one item on our lists was in our possession waiting to be packed. I was waiting on the .325 rifle.

I had no doubt that our host would follow through with getting the gun into my hands in plenty of time to get familiar with it before the hunt, but I wasn't exactly sure when it would arrive. As I waited, I prepared myself for being behind a gun that might have a kick harder than I was used to. *Will the .325 take meat on both ends of the barrel? Would the surgery repair on my right shoulder be undone with one shot?* And when I mentally rehearsed using such a whopping load, the reason it was necessary haunted me. I kept asking, *Just how big are those brownies in Alaska?* I had a feeling the pictures didn't do justice to the way they looked in person and up close.

I won't forget the day my cell phone buzzed and the caller ID showed it was our host calling. Every time he did, it seemed the news only got better. He told me the .325 would soon arrive in Tennessee, cased and bore sighted.

When I went to pick it up, I couldn't believe how heavy-duty the travel case was. The combination weighed at least twenty pounds, which made me wonder, *What kind of barreled beast am I taking home with me?* As I opened the three very stout latches and raised the lid, I felt a little nervous. I wasn't sure what I was about to see.

Resting snugly in a specially cut and fitted foam form was the long-awaited rifle. *Whoa!* It sported a black composite stock, a nickel steel barrel topped with an expensive scope that had a wide-diameter eye-piece. What an incredible sight! I stared at it for a few seconds to take in the thrill. I shut it up, stowed it in my vehicle, and headed home.

When I got back to my house, I removed the rifle from its bed as if I were lifting a baby out of a crib. I could tell by the initial feel that it was a brute built for a brute. I removed the scope lens covers and raised the gun slowly to the firing position. The forend felt noticeably fatter in my left hand than that of my .270. I couldn't help but smile when the stock butt fit snugly into my right shoulder and my right eye was perfectly aligned with the scope. It was as if I'd been personally fitted for the gun. *How did they know*?

When I peered through the scope at a tree in our backyard, I didn't see a tree. I saw a monster brown bear standing broadside, staring at me, not sure of the form he saw and wondering whether to escape or attack. I smiled again—sort of.

When the two boxes of .325 Short Mag cartridges arrived, I flipped the end lid open on one of them. As I slid the Styrofoam, twenty-round holder out of the box, my eyes widened. I'd hunted a long time and loaded my share of smaller bore rifles, but until that moment I'd never seen such a "healthy" cartridge. It seemed as big around as my thumb.

I pinched one of the bullets by its base, pulled it out, held it nose up in front of me, and spoke to it. "You look mean!"

I was glad no one was standing nearby to hear me talk to a bullet. It wouldn't be the last time I mumbled to myself and to the rifle as I handled it. I had a few more things to say when I fired it for the first time.

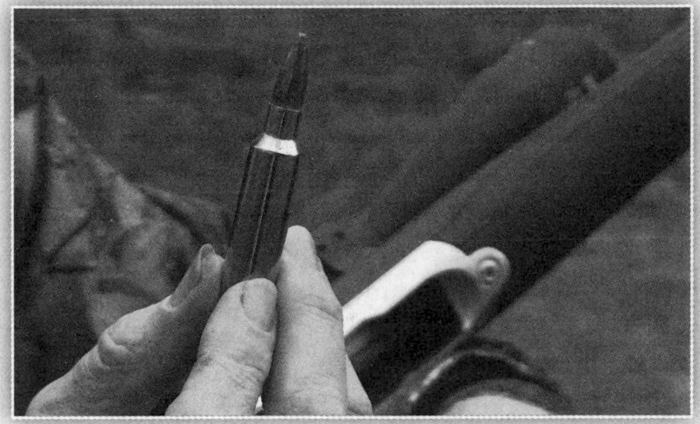

The beefy .325 Short Mag cartridge

I called Lindsey and told him I had the gun and would be heading to a farm near him the next day to try it out. He agreed to meet me there, take a few pictures, and record my first shoulder kiss with the rifle.

He was curious. "How's the gun feel?"

"I like it a ton and it feels like it was made for me, but I'm a little concerned about the brutality it's gonna render when I pull the trigger."

Lindsey laughed. "Hey, man, didn't you tell me a few years back when I first got into hunting, 'You won't feel a thing if you're shootin' at a deer'? A big ol' brown bear won't be any different!"

I thanked my friend for the timely reminder and hoped I would find out that I was making more of the anticipated kick than was necessary.

At the farm the next day, I set up a table, chair, and beanbag rests for my first firing. I walked off fifty yards and slid the two, stiff-wire feet of my stand-up target into the soft ground. Lindsey filmed me as I loaded the four-bullet clip. I was glad he didn't do a close-up of my hands. They were a little shaky.

Finally, I sat down, laid the rifle on my shooting tray/beanbag combination rest, and looked over the scope at the black-and-orange, splatter-type target out in the field. Slowly I slid the bolt back, pushed a bullet into the chamber, and looked at Lindsey as if saying, "It was nice knowing you." I felt for the safety. With ear protection on, I nuzzled my eye near the scope, put the safety in the Off position, laid my finger carefully on the trigger guard, found the center of the target, put the crosshairs right on it, took in a deep breath—and then looked up and said, "Lindsey, you first!"

He laughed.

I knew that sooner or later I would have to "connect" with the .325 and get used to it, so I looked through the scope, held the crosshairs on the mark, moved my finger to the trigger, and silently coached myself onward. I put a little pressure on the trigger and…lifted my finger off the trigger. I returned the safety to the On position and stood up. "I have a little neck pillow in the truck I need to get."

Shoulder shock!

"What for?"

Lindsey knew what for!

"To put between the stock and my precious shoulder, dude."

Lindsey shook his head and grinned as I retrieved the camo-covered pillow and carried it to the shooting table. It was shaped sort of like a dog bone.

"Don't laugh, my friend. I need the comfort—and the confidence that comes with it."

I pushed my ear plugs in tighter, settled back into the firing position with my eye at the scope. I found the target, set the crosshairs on the center mark, made sure there was no barrel movement, took the safety off, fingered the trigger, inhaled a deep breath, and said, "Fire in the hole!" so Lindsey would brace himself with the camera as I took the shot.

One moment I was a man facing the fear of a rifle kick, the next moment I was living a movie scene—the one in *A Christmas Story* where little Ralphie got punched in the shoulder by the mean, red-headed bully, Scut Farkus. I was Ralphie, and the .325 was Farkus. I wanted to say more about the punch I'd just endured, but all I said was, "*Whoa!*"

As I sat back and processed what had just happened, I realized one thing I'd forgotten to do. I'd failed to imagine a brown bear as the target so the kick wouldn't be so intense. Well, it was intense.

As the echo of the blast faded and my eyes stopped jiggling, I looked at Lindsey. "Still alive!" I said.

"Where did it hit?" Lindsey was thinking clearly, but I wasn't.

"My shoulder!"

"No, on the target."

"Oh…" I picked up my binoculars and looked at the target. "Two inches high and slightly to the right of the bull's eye. Good spot for fifty yards. Dead bear. I need to fire another round to make sure it wasn't pilot error."

I evaluated my body's response to the shot and realized that even though it was noticeable, the shoulder pressure had been tolerable. *Did I over-imagine and overestimate the kicking power of the gun? Did the little shock-absorbing pillow on my shoulder give me a false reading on the "Farkus effect" I thought I'd feel?* For whatever reason, I didn't hurt—and I was relieved. The dread of firing the other nineteen bullets in the box was gone. It was time to get serious about familiarizing myself with the gun and making sure it consistently put a hole where I aimed.

The second shot at fifty yards was better than the first. I felt good about moving the target to 100 yards. With each of the next five shots I whispered, "Dead bear," when I saw where the bullet hit. My confidence level was now up seven percent (a percentage point for each bullet).

I decided to let the barrel cool down a little while. I stood and went to my truck. Opening the box in the bed, I pulled out the clothes I planned to wear hunting. I put on the long johns, under sweater, waders, heavy coat, and toboggan hat. I wanted to know how the gun felt when I shot it wearing the bulky gear. A few rounds later, I was feeling even better about the fit of the rifle.

I decided to try something I'd seen on a video made by a professional hunter who offered some tips on preparing for brown bear hunting. He'd suggested running far and fast enough to get winded and then stop, quickly get the gun into firing position while imagining a bear in the scope's field of view, find the sweet spot, and take the shot. The purpose for this exercise was to be prepared to shoot while the heart rate is elevated due to the hurried stalk, the adrenaline, and more importantly, an angry bear approaching quickly. I called it my "duress rehearsal."

Doing the run for "duress" rehearsal

The next four shots using this method were pitiful in terms of placement. The hole pattern in the target looked shotgun-ish. I knew I needed more work with the run-and-shoot training exercise. It took a few more sweaty attempts, but I finally felt like I could hit the mark after a run/drop/shoot situation. As for the attacking bear shot, I really hoped I wouldn't have to face that.

In two trips to the farm, I shot through the two boxes of shells my host had provided. I called several gun stores in my area, but none of them carried the 220-grain, .325 Short Mag bullet that my host said would be best for a big bear. I did an online search and found them at a site that thought a lot of their cartridges. The sticker shock was more noticeable than the butt shock of the gun on my shoulder. At nearly three dollars per bullet, I thought about ordering a single box of twenty, consider myself ready for the hunt gun-wise, and save my dollars. Thankfully, better judgment kicked in. It wouldn't be wise to risk readiness just for the sake of cash. After placing two separate orders, I'd invested in four boxes of .325s. It was the right thing to do, but forking out the funds made me hold the gun a lot steadier when I practiced.

11

Waiting Wisely

"Don't take the shell off of your pet snail—it'll just make him sluggish."

When it came to waiting until I left Tennessee to go to Alaska, time was definitely a snail that had its shell ripped off. Gathering the gear and getting familiar with the .325 rifle had occupied a lot of thought time and carried me through Christmas, but I still had more than four months to wait for the May 9 departure date. It was painful. The only thing that helped me deal with the sluggish movement of the hands on the clock was to continue to prepare.

The following is a list of other things besides gear gathering that needed to be done in advance of the trip. Included with some items are the details involved.

- ✓ Secure airline reservations. (It's Alaska, a state that tourists love. Don't wait to get a seat on a plane. The final destination for our flight was Sitka, Alaska. Arrival on May 9 in the afternoon or evening, and a return to Tennessee 12 days later on the first available flight out. Use frequent flyer miles, and if there's not enough in my account, beg Annie for hers. Surely, she wouldn't mind.)
- ✓ Check on lodging. (Landing on May 9 and the boat departing on May 11 meant two nights' lodging upon arrival. Add

a night when the boat returns the evening before our flight departure the next morning. Total number of nights for lodging—three. Thankfully, Lindsey and I can share a room and share the cost. Surely Annie and Susan will be happy with our sacrifice.)

✓ Before completing and signing the hunting application sent by the guide, watch the *Take a Closer Look* video online that's required by the Alaska Department of Fish and Game. (The purpose of the video is to help hunters and wildlife watchers accurately identify the gender of brown and grizzly bears. Watching the clips must be done so that the box on the application can be checked to indicate that it was viewed. If I was in the unplanned situation where I had to choose whether or not a bear was legal without the keen and helpful eyes of an experienced guide, I wanted to make the right choice. Not only was it a very important component of the hunt preparation, but it was enjoyable to see the bears in their habitat. The clips showing the wide-faced, broad-shouldered bears lumbering down the shoreline made my trigger finger twitch.)

✓ Finish filling out the application, check it over, check it again, sign it, and send it back to the guide. Slipping the envelope through the "Put mail here" slot in the box at our local post office was a memorable moment. As I let go of it, I thought about the nearly 3000 miles the envelope would travel. I was envious but took comfort knowing I wouldn't be that far behind.

✓ Practice with the .325, take the full set of clothing for the "duress rehearsal" and fire more of those pricy bullets. (My musically talented son believes that when it comes to performing, "If you want anywhere near 100 percent from yourself on stage, you have to practice 200 percent." The same is true about "performing" a shot on the big stage of the outdoors. Hunters refer to it as "the moment of truth" because it reveals whether we're ready.)

✓ Order more bullets!

✓ Find a really good hiding place at our house for storing the .325 in its case. (Annie and I had concert and seminar events to do during the months prior to the hunt. Because our trips take us away from home for days at a time, I felt the weight of responsibility in regard to protecting the expensive gun that had been placed in my care. My other guns were of great value to me too, but holding another man's highly regarded and costly weapon, especially if it's for his grandson, drove me to even greater security measures. In the end, I felt pretty good about where and how well I concealed the weapon.)

✓ Connect with other hunters who had been to Alaska in pursuit of bear and pick their brains about their experiences. (One thing I discovered as I sought advice from guys who had hunted Alaskan bear was that they loved to bring up the dangerous aspects of it just to see if they could make sweat break out on the foreheads of newbies. For example, in January I went to Montana to speak at a wild game dinner event. During lunch with the planning staff, I mentioned that I had my first-ever Alaska brown bear hunt coming up in May.

  One of the men said, "Oh yeah. Been there and survived that!"

  I looked across the table at him and hoped he couldn't tell that I'd swallowed hard. "Survived?" I asked. "Do you think it's not a safe thing to do?"

  He smiled and delivered the line he'd set me up for. "Oh, sure, most people who go bear hunting in Alaska come back alive."

  I laughed—sort of.)

The various tips I gleaned from the few hunters I talked to were valuable indeed.

- Be prepared to feel a lot of wet and cold.
- Don't be stupid and wander away from your guide.
- Take extra ammo in your daypack.

- You'll be super hyped if you're aiming at a bear, so make sure you don't make the mistake of aiming at his silhouette instead of at a spot on him.
- If you're sitting on an island beach waiting on a bear to come to you, position yourself so you can easily and often look both ways.

I appreciated the input from those I spoke to and was sure I'd hear more sage advice from our host and the guide when we got to Alaska. But perhaps this insight I got from a seasoned hunter was the best.

> Not everyone who goes to Alaska after a brownie or a grizzly will get to pull the trigger. It's a fact of life. Sometimes it's because you simply don't see a taker boar, sometimes you only see females, and sometimes you don't see anything at all. But whether or not you see a bear, whatever you do, see the territory. Take it all in. It's massive, it's awesome, and most importantly, it'll make the One who created it seem even bigger. And He deserves to be bigger in your heart.

Sunset in Alaska

12

Arrival of Departure Day

During the winter months leading up to the departure to Alaska, not a day passed that I didn't think about what was ahead. I was like a little boy waiting in line at an ice-cream truck. My turn couldn't come fast enough. Lindsey felt the same way. When we'd see each other at church or other places, the first thing we'd talk about was how many days until the magical month of May arrived.

Then, as if we weren't already antsy enough to go, an item came in the mail that put our anticipation in overdrive. It was a DVD…a homemade documentary of one of our host's previous hunts. It showed the guide, his boat, the very dock we'd be standing on to board it, his crew, scenes of some of the area we'd be sailing, and best of all, brown bear hunting action. I watched it enough that I thought the laser in the DVD player would start a fire and melt the disc. As far as I was concerned, the film deserved an Otter (my version of an Oscar) for best outdoor film of the year.

While the winter weeks slogged by like refrigerated molasses poured from a jar, thankfully there was another distraction that would help Lindsey and me tolerate the wait. If anything could effectively draw our attention away from May 9, it was April 1. That was the day spring gobbler season opened in Tennessee.

The first morning of legally hunting since the close of deer season in early January kept my mind very busy. It required dusting off and roughing up the slate calls, rechalking the box calls, relearning how not to gag while using mouth calls (at least for me), and transferring the pruning snips and handsaw from the deer hunting pack to the turkey hunting vest. So much to do while scouting, plotting, and scheming where to be sitting when sunrise woke the birds up on April 1.

There were two things that turkey hunting season reminded us of that served us well in Alaska. One was the need to be patient. We had learned on more occasions than we care to admit what happens when we don't outwait a gobbler we think is coming in. Giving up and standing up too soon taught us over and over that if we don't give the tom a chance, all we're going to take home from the hunt is the memory of the gobbler's nervous, unhappy, warning cluck that he makes when impatient humans reveal their presence. If we had a dollar for every time our shoulders drooped in disappointment at the sudden sound and sad sight of a sneaky long beard bolting because we moved to soon, we'd have enough cash to pay for the therapy needed to help us get over it.

We decided it would definitely be good for the bear hunt to take a refresher course in patience during turkey season. For the sake of not rendering bodily harm to one another while afield with a weapon, a review of gun safety while turkey hunting was beneficial. Nothing can ruin a good hunt like a hole in a buddy's body caused by a gun that discharged because the safety wasn't on. As the one who would be carrying a .325 in Alaska, I desperately didn't want to be guilty of that mistake.

As a matter of confession, I hold a memory of a near disaster that made it even more critical that I spend a month checking my safety button on my gun while chasing gobblers. With a half-day to hunt, I went solo to a farm. Before daylight, I loaded my pump-action twelve-gauge and excitedly headed away from my truck to the field where I hoped the flock would fly when they dropped off their roost. I set up at the edge of the grassy meadow under a big oak tree. Sunrise came and went with no birds in sight. I heard gobbling in the distance and decided to abandon my set up and begin a chase.

I spent the next three hours running, crawling, and setting up several times. As hard as I tried to get within range of a strutter, it didn't happen. I walked back to my truck, removed my camo mask, and started to unload my shotgun. That's when the blood ran from my head to my feet. I no doubt looked ashen when I realized I'd spent almost four hours wandering the hills with the gun safety in the off position.

I replayed the morning in my mind. The thought of how many times the barrel was pointed at my foot or my leg while pressing through underbrush and trotting through stump-laden woods gave me chills. How easily a twig or my wayward finger could have pressed the trigger and turned a good day into a really bad and bloody one. Lesson learned—and how glad I was that I was the only one in class that day.

The thirty days of Tennessee gobbler season were indeed good for both a mental diversion and a timely review of hunting tactics and ethics. We took a couple of nice birds and made it to May without incident.

Wow! The longed-for month had arrived at last. Only nine more sleeps!

I woke up early on May 9, got dressed, got Annie up to get ready to take me to the airport, and then headed to my man cave where my three bags waited to be put in our van. On top of the very tightly packed, brown canvas, 40-inch-long duffel bag was my checklist. I'd placed it there the night before—after going over it carefully one last time before attempting to get some sleep. Still, I checked it again that morning.

There was one thing on my mental list that was not written on the paper. I'd called my dad the evening before to see how he was doing. I wanted to make sure he was feeling well enough for me to basically disappear for twelve days. He assured me he was okay. I had my mother write down the landline number for the guide's office in case they needed to get in touch with me and Annie wasn't available. It was a sobering phone call, and when I hung up I whispered a prayer for both Dad's and Mom's well-being while I was away.

Satisfied that all the items on the list were inside the designated bags, the gun case latches and locks were secure, the keys to the padlocks were in my pocket where they should be, and my flight tickets and ID were handy, I carried everything to the van. It was sort of surreal that every movement was for the purpose of completing the 2616-mile journey to Sitka. As we pulled out of our driveway, I thought, *If all goes well, by nine tonight* (after midnight in Tennessee) *I'll be stepping on Sitka, Alaska, soil!* I was giddy.

I met Lindsey at the Nashville Airport ninety minutes before departure. The extra time was needed in case we had to deal with delays related to checking in a rifle. At passenger unloading, we kissed and hugged our sweet and understanding wives goodbye, turned our hearts northwest (as if they weren't already headed in that direction), and walked into the terminal. Thankfully, there was no trouble checking in the heavy gun and case, as well as my obese duffel bag. Lindsey's bags were acceptable as well. We then headed to the TSA station. Once we were on the other side of security, we agreed that at last we were officially on our way. Our steps were light as we headed to our gate.

It was music to our ears when we heard, "We're now boarding the flight to Salt Lake City." It was our first of three stops before landing in Sitka. As I walked behind Lindsey down the aisle of the plane wearing my heavy camo coat, I wanted to tell everyone where I was going. Unfortunately, no one asked—except for a flight attendant who stopped at my seat and gave me a chance to share my joy.

"Goin' huntin'?" she asked.

"Yes, ma'am!"

"Where?"

"Alaska!" I smiled as I said it.

"What are you going for?"

"Brown bear."

Her face showed concern as she said, "Oh my. Do be careful."

"Oh, don't worry about me, ma'am. It's this guy you need to worry about." I pointed at Lindsey.

"Why?" she asked.

"'Cause he's going with me, and I can outrun him."

The joke worked again.

As I buckled up, I looked out the window and could see the luggage conveyor. I watched the process long enough to see that every piece of our baggage, including the rifle, was loaded onto the belt. So far so good.

The flight attendant closed the front door, and I felt the familiar vibration of jet engines starting. As the volume grew to a roar, I thought, *No turning back now, bubba. All systems go!* Then, as the realization hit me that the first day of my adventure would include about twelve hours in potentially dangerous and unpredictable air travel, the second verse of a song came to mind. It was a song Lindsey and I had written a few months earlier that addressed a sobering fact of life, one that was made extra real the moment the engines of the plane came to life. When you read the verse about an airplane ride, you'll know what I was feeling.

You Just Never Know

He gets in the car, radio on
Driving to work at the break of dawn
All at once up ahead a car overturns
He's first on the scene as it starts to burn
No time for thinking, life on the line
Now that Mom and her baby are gonna be fine

Oh, you just never know what a day will bring
No way to know, till it's happening
You can plan, you can scheme,
You can hope, you can dream
But till the day comes and goes,
You just never know

She gets on the plane, she takes her seat
She calls home before it's time to leave
Tells her husband, "I'll be landing at noon...
Can't wait to hold you, I'll see you soon."
Then she bows her head as the big engines start
She whispers a prayer and crosses her heart

'Cause you just never know what a day will bring
No way to know, till it's happening
You can plan, you can scheme, you can hope, you can
dream
But till the day comes and goes
You just never know

Sometimes life will lift up your soul
Sometimes life can lay you low
Not much is certain, but one thing is clear
You'll never live in the moment till it gets here
You just never know what a day will bring[1]

Regretfully, I'd waited too long to call Annie on my cell to say another goodbye. I did, however, bow my head and whisper a prayer that God would protect us and let us hold each other again. Ten minutes later, the wheels lifted off the Tennessee ground, and the plane made a sweeping westward turn. We were dream bound.

13

The Bear in the Glass Box

After six hours of traveling from Nashville to Salt Lake City to Seattle, we had a two-hour layover. Then we boarded our flight to Juneau, our first touchdown in Alaska! As I settled into my seat, I silently laughed at myself about how going to hunt in the great state of Alaska had distracted me from my dislike of flying. Though I'm totally intrigued by aviation and the amazing technology that goes with it, I'm not a huge fan of crawling into a long aluminum tube and allowing my body to be propelled at hundreds of miles per hour. I do it because my work requires it, but I don't like the idea of calling airports *terminals*. It's sick humor. To make it worse, they ask questions like, "What's your *final* destination?" Even sicker.

Thankfully, the skies were calm as we flew, and the bird we were in seemed plenty strong. Because we were traveling west, we kept gaining hours, seemingly going back in time. For that reason, it was still daylight when we finally made it over Alaska territory. I watched Lindsey as he stared at the awesome, mountainous scenery below. He couldn't take his eyes off it. Neither could I. We were thrilled to get this visual of the Last Frontier.

Alaska is indeed a sight to behold. As the northernmost and westernmost state, it covers a massive 663,268 square miles, which is more than twice the size of Texas. In fact, with all its land mass and territorial waterways, Alaska is bigger than Texas, Montana, and California combined. For that reason, when people ask Annie and me if we've traveled overseas to minister through music and speaking, we smile and say, "Why would we want to do that? We haven't covered Alaska yet!"

Declared a state in January of 1959, Alaska has a population today of approximately 750,000 people, per the 2010 census. It has nearly 34,000 miles of shoreline, 3 million lakes, 16,000 square miles of glacier ice, and is peppered with several active volcanoes. It also boasts the highest mountain peak in North America—Denali, also known as Mount McKinley. Rising 20,310 feet above sea level, it demands the admiration of everyone who sees it. To some adventurous (perhaps crazy) souls, it whispers, "Just come and try to conquer me." And they do—by the thousands.

Alaska wildlife is spectacular. The nonhuman residents of the millions of acres of land are the mighty brown, black, and polar bears, caribou, moose, mountain goat, bison, Dall sheep, bald eagles, owls, osprey, sandhill cranes, and ravens. The inland lakes and the seas that border the territory are filled with humpback, bowhead, fin, and blue whales as well as striped dolphins, sea lions, turtles, otters, and species of fish too numerous to list. We were heading to the biggest unfenced zoo in the world.

When we got within range of the Juneau Airport, we could see a couple of cruise ships docked near downtown and dozens of small floatplanes sitting on the water. It was a different world. When we landed, Lindsey and I did a knuckle bump to congratulate each other for finally stepping on Alaskan concrete. It had been a long time coming, but our journey wasn't over. One more flight was ahead.

The layover in Juneau was nearly an hour, so we took the flight crew up on their offer to exit the plane. While inside the terminal, we saw something that made our jaws drop. Contained in a huge display box made of thick, clear Plexiglass was a taxidermy mount of a massive brown bear. I studied the anatomy of the boar and thought about the shot placement photos I had reviewed in preparation for the hunt. Chills ran up and down my spine at the thought that I might encounter one of his kind in the ten days to come. It was sobering to say the least, but I was also excited. I felt ready for the challenge!

Before I walked away from the display, I couldn't stop myself from pretending to raise the .325 to my shoulder, finding the bear's vitals in the imaginary scope, and pulling the invisible trigger. The make-believe shot gave me shivers of anticipation. What would the real deal feel like? I couldn't wait to find out.

Bear in a glass case at Juneau airport

14

Sitka at Last!

We boarded the plane again in Juneau to complete the all-day journey. My body was tired, but I felt a surge of energy as the flight plan to our destination took us over the massive Admiralty Island, the smaller Catherine Island, innumerable and majestic snow-capped mountains, and the incredibly beautiful bays that were wide and as blue as indigo.

The sun was setting in Sitka as we made the Saturday evening approach to the local airport. With the sky's various hues of pink, maroon, gray, and soft white reflecting on the waterways that led to the town, Lindsey and I nearly broke our necks as we looked wide-eyed through the window of the plane. The scene was as enthralling as we'd imagined.

When we touched down and taxied to the gate, I wondered if all of our baggage was in the belly of the bird we were on. *What about our duffel bags filled with all things necessary for the hunt? And the heavy rifle? Did they all make it here?* Though the trip was now complete and nothing could be done about any problems, I still prayed, *Lord, let our bags show up too!* And hallelujah, they did!

As we were heaving our tightly packed, weighty bags off the conveyer belt in baggage claim, I heard a familiar voice.

Our host said, "You made it! Welcome to Alaska!"

What a joy to turn around and see his smiling face. There was a distinct twinkle in his eyes as he spoke. I knew he was excited about watching a couple of total newbies take in the awesome thrill of an Alaskan hunting experience just as he'd done several years earlier. He was well acquainted with how uniquely thrilling the following days would be for us. The knowledge was ringing his happy bell.

Dale Adams, Alaska guide

"This is Lindsey Williams," I said. Lindsey's first words to our host as they shook hands were, "Thank you, thank you, thank you for this opportunity!" Lindsey's gratitude was graciously received with a "you're very welcome" grin from our host. Then he turned and introduced two men who were standing right behind him.

"Meet Jason. He's the other trigger guy on the hunt."

Jason grinned as we shook his hand and jokingly warned him that we'd been to the track before leaving for Alaska and were confident that both of us could run faster than he could. He pointed out the fact that he was taller than either of us, so his legs were longer...plus he was about ten years younger. We all laughed—sort of.

Our host put his hand out toward the second man standing with him and said, "Meet Mr. Dale Adams. He's our guide and owner of the service he calls Adams Alaskan Safaris."

Dale towered above all of us, and his very in-shape build suggested he was not a stranger to hard work. He put his hand out to shake mine, and I could feel the ruggedness of the Last Frontier in his grip. Suddenly I felt safer.

Dale Adams was a well-mannered gentleman, and at this first meeting he didn't say a whole lot other than how glad he was that we'd arrived. I appreciated his friendly welcome and assumed that he was a somewhat quiet personality who, though extremely skilled as a guide, would not be much of conversationalist. Man, was I wrong.

15

The Unforgettable Guide

As we got to know Dale Adams, we discovered that instead of being a man of few words as we'd thought at first, he was filled to the brim with entertaining conversation. We wouldn't know how willing and ready he was to share it with us until the next day, and for a good reason.

Because it was the season for hunting bear in Alaska, our group wasn't the only one he would guide that spring. When we met him at the airport, he'd just come back that morning from an all-night cruise to Sitka after completing a multiday bear hunt with another pair of hunters. It had ended with a last-day kill that required a later-than-normal return. He was a tired boy. No wonder he was initially quiet. Lindsey and I had no idea what all he'd done that day. Here's what he later shared about his Saturday.

- May 9, midnight: Pull anchor and begin the all-night cruise back to Sitka.
- Five to seven hours (depending on the weather) of staying awake, checking more weather reports, carefully navigating through some tight spots in the inlets, making sure the boat didn't suffer damage from floating debris—and all in the deep darkness of the Alaskan night. The safe return of all passengers was his top priority.

- Arrive at his personal dock section around seven or eight in the morning, moor the boat securely, write all activities in his logbook, assist the well-rested hunters off the boat, and escort them to the airport or their lodging.
- Refill the 1800-gallon, freshwater holding tank.
- Prepare a bear cape (the hide) for shipment to a hunter's address, which requires filling out forms and tending to other legal matters.
- Oversee the cleaning of the boat.
- Fill the 3000-gallon fuel tank.
- Do necessary maintenance on the main engine, generator, navigation equipment, fishing gear, and anything else that needs it.
- Go to the local grocer to buy food, drinks, snacks, and so on for the next hunting group to enjoy.
- Stop at the local ice vendor to get twenty bags of ice (fifty pounds each) to keep the daily catch of seafood cool and, hopefully, chill another bear cape or two.
- Go to his house and catch up on emails, postal mail, and other business matters that required attention, especially messages from future clients.
- Somewhere along the way, eat something.
- Finally, get in the truck and go to the airport to meet a couple of bug-eyed, uncontrollably excited, and "completely unaware of how much work it takes to be a hunting-guide" dudes from Tennessee. He would smile, appear to be enthusiastic, and hope we didn't notice his tiredness and few words.

So that was pretty much the day Dale Adams had just lived when we met him, and yet he was friendly when he greeted us. I wouldn't understand until the end of our time with him what a trooper he really was on our behalf. I have nothing but good to say about him, including his excellent demeanor, disciplined actions, and outstanding professionalism. I thought of the time years ago when I had dreamed of making a living the way Dale Adams was. In high school and with a mere two or three years into being a hunter, I would read outdoor magazines and watch the one television outdoor show we got. I noticed that in each form of media, a hunting guide was usually in the cast of characters. As I would read about them and watch them lead hunters to their trophies, I would think, *Wow, wouldn't it be incredible to do that for a living!*

Eventually, the idea of becoming a hunting guide so intrigued me that I set my sights on the day when I could do it. My goal was to graduate from high school, work to earn enough money to buy a bus ticket to a state like Colorado, Montana, or Idaho, and head west to become a hunting guide.

I was also the poster boy for naivety. I had absolutely no idea what would be required to make guiding my life's vocation. All I wanted to do was hunt and be with other hunters. Because I never shared this goal with anyone, including Kenneth Bledsoe, I gave no one a chance to tell me the facts of a guide's life. I now concede that it was a good thing that guiding didn't pan out. God had other steps for me to walk. The following song lyric tells a story similar to mine and definitely reveals the feelings I have about my life journey.

The Huntin' Guide

His high school classroom felt like prison walls when
November came
'Cause it's hard to hear your teacher talk when a deer
stand calls your name
At night he'd read his *Field & Stream*—it was back in 1962
The stories and the pictures fed a young hunter's dreams
He knew exactly what he wanted to do

He said, "Someday I'm gonna go out West
Where the mountains kiss the sky
I'll make a name, I'm gonna be the best, they'll come to me
I'm gonna be a hunting guide"

He said, "If I can just make it till next spring, I'll wear
that cap and gown
Then I'll go out West, and climb up in those Rockies,
and maybe never come back down"

But in September of his senior year, something woke
him from his dreams
He said he'd never seen a finer deer—her name was
Mary Jean
And on that day his western plans began to drift back east
It's strange how love can change a man, guess it can tame
even the wildest beast

Thirty seasons have come and gone, and he still loves my
mother, Mary Jean
But as we hunt together on this November dawn, he
talks again about that dream
I see regrets in his eyes like that morning mist that paints
the wheat field gray
But when my shot connects in the distance, I see that
sadness go away
He says…
"Oh, I think you got him, son. Wish you could see your face
It's amazing how we can feel so close in such a wide-
open space"

So I said, "Dad, remember back when I was younger
I left home and went out hunting for the truth?
And for a while I wandered on over to the dark side of
my youth
But I couldn't forget how I felt so safe with you
When I was in the woods by your side
And you're the reason I came back home; you led me to
the Trophy of Grace
You've been my soul's hunting guide

Oh, Dad, I'm glad you didn't go out West where the
mountains kiss the sky
I would have never known you are the best, and I thank you
For being my hunting guide
You're leading me to heaven, Dad, and I thank you
For being my hunting guide"[2]

It takes a strong man with a special set of skills to do what Dale Adams does. Over the next ten days, I watched him work until exhausted, joyfully entertain his clients, and expertly guide our bear hunts. I became keenly aware of the fact that I didn't possess the attributes he owned. God had gifted him in a way that He didn't gift me. How thankful I am to have met a man who confirmed that reality for me.

I went to sleep that night in our Sitka hotel room unaware that Dale's day wasn't over yet. It was nearing midnight, and he still had more emails to answer, more mail from the post office to open, bills to pay, and another voyage to plan. Just a day in the life of a hunting guide.

Dale—always huntin'

16

Sunday in Sitka

Because of the time zone difference between Tennessee and Alaska, when Lindsey and I finally hit the sack on Saturday near midnight, it was around three in the morning "body time." We felt the tiring effects of a long day of flying and thought we would immediately pass into deep slumber. That didn't happen for one simple reason: We were keyed up from the excitement of arriving in brown bear country.

For about twenty minutes we lay in our beds in the darkness and talked about how strange it was to have traveled so far from home without using our passports, the shivers of anticipation the bear in the glass cage gave us, and how much we looked forward to taking photos of awesome Sitka scenes when daylight came. As we talked, I noticed Lindsey's voice was getting lower with more space between exchanges. Then there was a long pause after I said something. Five seconds later, I heard the familiar sound of intermittent snoring. It wasn't loud and annoying, thankfully, but it did inform me that I was left talking to myself.

Instead of recounting more details of the day, as enjoyable as they were, my thoughts turned to what our host had planned for my Sunday in Sitka. Knowing I was a songwriter and performer, he'd called a few weeks prior to the trip to ask if it would be acceptable if he arranged for me to share a few songs at the church where our guide's family attended. I had no objections. In fact, I was so grateful for the chance to go hunting with him, singing at the church was the least I could do. If he had asked, I would have also washed every car in the parking lot during Sunday school!

My participation was to span about twenty minutes prior to the pastor's sermon. Because I consider every opportunity given to me to sing and speak to be a serious responsibility from God, especially in church settings, there was one question that kept me awake. *Of all the things I could say to a congregation that I'll likely speak to only once in my life, what could possibly be the most helpful in terms of their spiritual journey?*

Before I joined Lindsey in Snoretown, I knew what my message would be. I would especially make sure I included the song "The Secret Place." I consider it to be the most important lyric I've ever written. It's a simple, country-style song that compares the human heart to a house. It reveals the importance of being willing to open every room in the "home of our heart" to God—even the rooms that are filled with things we'd rather He didn't see. This was something I'd personally done years earlier and continue to do. Because I'd experienced the peace of mind that comes with being open and honest with God, I was hopeful that sharing my experience with the congregation would help people want to know the same peace. With that goal in mind, I finally drifted off to sleep.

The alarm on our phones roused us at seven, and by eight we were dressed and ready to go meet with the folks who attended Sitka Christian Center. Along with our host and Jason, Lindsey and I rode with Dale to the church. We rendezvoused there with Lori, Dale's wife and hardworking partner in their guide business.

As the attendees gathered in the sanctuary, my concern that I had not brought my "Sunday go to meetin'" clothes was erased. I discovered I fit right in. I was in Alaska, where fancy was not required when it came to church attire. The only expectation in terms of covering was decency. These were my kind of folks. For the record, I removed my baseball cap when I entered the sanctuary—mainly because Annie would have demanded it.

The service began with some energetic congregational singing, heartfelt prayers, and Scripture reading. Then an introduction was given for Lindsey and me. We walked to the front of the church, picked up two borrowed guitars, and turned to face the group. I had stood before thousands of audiences and calmly done full-length concerts. But I felt nervous in Sitka. I didn't want to fumble through my songs and comments and distract from the message I wanted to share. I also didn't want to embarrass my new friend Dale, who had stuck his neck out when suggesting to the church staff that I sing.

I quickly scanned the room and was set at ease when I saw smiles that were warm and welcoming to a pair of Tennessee strangers. I said a few words to introduce myself and Lindsey, and then we started picking the intro to the first song. Heads started nodding—and not for sleeping, I'm happy to say. The room felt friendly, and every word seemed to be received with gratitude.

Singing in Sitka

I ended my part with "The Secret Place," as I'd felt I should do. I heard a few affirming amens as we strummed the last chord. I glanced at Dale and saw that he was smiling. Mission accomplished! My hopes that he would be pleased appeared to be met. Even better, I'd encouraged some Alaskan pilgrims with the comforting truth found in Philippians 1:6: "He who began a good work in you will perfect it until the day of Christ Jesus." And, to put it in Tennessee terms, "God loves us enough to accept us the way we are when we come to Him, but He loves us even more by not leaving us that way."

After some meet-and-greet time following dismissal at the church, we headed to lunch. Over some very tasty Alaskan pizza, we talked about the all-day voyage up the coast that would begin the next morning. The conversation didn't last long enough in my estimation because the more we strategized, the more my trigger finger twitched. I was in hog heaven with this group.

We piled into Dale's pickup truck and headed to the local hardware and outdoor gear store. Though it was Sunday, the doors were open and the aisles were filled with shoppers. The line at the checkout counter was deep, mostly with men buying everything from fishing tackle to dog food. We were there for one item—the rain gloves our host had mentioned in his list of things we'd need for the hunt.

We found the shelf that held the orange-colored, heavy rubber gloves and tried them on. I was quite surprised at how instantly warm the wool lining felt. I knew without a doubt that I'd be very glad to have the protection on my hands in the bitter cold Alaskan water and skin-pinching winds we'd face.

A harbor in legendary Sitka, Alaska

From the hardware store we drove a short distance to an ice warehouse. One chore Dale had not completed the day before was to get the fifty-pound bags of crushed ice for the trip. The four of us from the Lower Forty-Eight volunteered to help load the bags into Dale's truck. To make it quick and painless for him, we formed a conveyor line to get it done. As I passed bag after bag of ice down the line, I thought again about how much work a hunting guide does for the sake of the ones pulling the triggers.

Lindsey and I were on our own for the rest of the evening. We decided to bundle up and take a walk with the camera. It was time well spent because the photos taken were priceless. To this day, every time I look at them I go back to that Sunday in Sitka and thank God for every minute of my time in such a legendary town with such great people.

Boarding the Big Boat

In the first chapter of this book I said in reference to going to sleep the night before my first hunt in October of 1963, "I could not have known that it would be the last night in my life that I would go to sleep that easy before going hunting the next morning." It couldn't have been truer than when it was time to bed down on Sunday night in Sitka. I was super excited about getting up the next morning and boarding the big boat to go hunting. In order to get some shut-eye, I had to resort to counting more than sheep. I added deer, turkey, elk, antelope, and even some game wardens to the lineup.

Lindsey was just as antsy to head out as I was. He was beyond ready to capture the endless and incredible scenes that Alaska offered. While my trigger finger twitched in anticipation of taking a shot at a bear with the .325, his shutter-release finger was bouncing up and down, ready to hit the buttons on his Nikon. I had bullets to load in my gun; he had smart cards to load into his camera. Sleep didn't come easy, but it finally did.

When the alarm sounded just before dawn, we had no problem getting up. It's strange how quickly and willingly feet can hit the floor when hunting is in the schedule. Within a few minutes we were both in the hotel lobby, checking out of our room and looking forward to moving our things into the next room reserved for us.

An hour and a sausage biscuit later, we were piling out of Dale's pickup truck and toting duffel bags, shoulder bags, gun cases, and groceries down the long, narrow, wood-planked dock to the port side of the 64-foot, custom-built vessel named *Surveyor*. We wanted to take a minute to stand beside her and admire her giganticness, but it was "all hands on deck" to help move everyone's gear and other supplies off the dock and onto the aft deck of the boat.

When everything was on board, it was time to take in the glorious feeling of having the solid main deck of *Surveyor* under our boots. She was a stately "motor yacht" painted white. The fresh Navy-gray paint on her deck appeared clean enough to use as a dinner plate. We stood on her spacious, covered aft deck, looked her over, and commented on her well-maintained condition. A lot of nice things were said, and we hadn't even gone inside to see the rest of our floating accommodations.

When we stepped through the door, just to the right was a diesel-fueled, free-standing stove. Sitting on top was a fresh-brewed pot of some of the best coffee known to mankind. (Of course, even a cup of poor quality coffee will taste incredible when it's consumed on an immaculate sailing vessel headed for a hunting ground.)

Lindsey and I poured ourselves cups of the steaming, high-quality joe and checked out the galley, living, and dining areas we'd entered. I noticed that the cabinets, cubbyhole doors, window frames, and dinner table and booths were made of beautifully grained teak. Known as the king of woods, teak is preferred by most mariners because of its value and versatility. Without the need for painting and varnish, it's the only wood that can endure the brutally harsh seawater and the intense heat of the sun without splitting, warping, and cracking. There was so much of it just in the galley area that I wondered if there was any more to be had on the planet.

Dale stepped into the area and interrupted our admiration. "Guys, let me show you where you'll be bunking so you can bring your stuff in from the aft deck and settle in."

Surveyor had three staterooms forward of the galley. As we stepped down into the room Lindsey and I would occupy, I had a flashback to my two years on the aircraft carrier USS *Forrestal*. The quarters I occupied on that ship resembled those on *Surveyor*—compact but cozy.

Because I had the top bunk on the carrier, just for old time's sake I quickly called dibs on the top bunk in our stateroom.

As for the appearance of the sleeping quarters, we were surrounded with more teak. The bunk frames, closet door, and drawers were all faced with the honey-colored wood. I couldn't even begin to guess how many dollars' worth of teak I'd be sleeping on for the next ten days. I started to feel kingly in such regal surroundings.

With all our gear put away in our designated bunk areas, the rifles secured on the gun rack, and the cases stored below in a compartment aft of the engine room, Dale took a moment to introduce us to his right-hand man and assistant guide, Alex. I'd seen him working harder than all the rest of us as he prepared *Surveyor* for launch, but I hadn't realized who he was.

Nearing thirty years old and built as stout as his boss, he stood quietly as Dale told us Alex was an experienced bear guide, expert fisherman, and all-around good sailor who would have our best interest and safety in mind at all times. It was a comforting introduction to hear.

Alex shook our hands, and when I felt his strong grip, once again it was as though I had shaken the rugged hand of Alaska. I looked at him and imagined myself in his shoes—forty years younger, of course. To be honest, I wrestled for a moment with envy.

My thoughts were brought to a sudden halt when I felt a rumble beneath my boots. The vibration was caused by the huge, 365-horse diesel engine in *Surveyor*'s belly coming to life. Oh, what a feeling! We were nearing launch time.

Sure enough, Alex headed to the dock to untie the thick mooring ropes. As he did, the ship's cook for the journey, who happened to be Dale's wife, Lori, came aboard. She put a few things away in the galley and invited any of us who wanted to go topside to the pilothouse to make our way up the narrow, winding staircase. Our host and Jason remained on the aft deck while Lindsey and I joined Dale at the wheel of *Surveyor*.

As we entered the impressive, teak-walled pilothouse, it was breathtaking to see windows all the way around that provided a clear, well-elevated, 360-degree view. I turned to look through the aft windows and nearly spilled my coffee when I saw what was on the roof that covered the aft main deck. There were two well-built, fourteen-foot skiffs sitting side by side. They sported large, hand-guided Yamaha motors. Waiting to lift them off the roof and lower them into the water was a hefty crane with heavy-duty metal cable. The thought that I'd be climbing into one of them the next day for the purpose of hunting bear had me stoked in a major way.

Dale welcomed us to his control tower and then left his pilot chair, went to the port window of the pilothouse, and yelled to Alex, "All clear?"

"Yes, sir!"

Dale took his seat in the "big" chair and said to Lindsey and me, "Well, fellas, it's time to sail north!"

Meeting *Surveyor*

My heart pounded as Dale throttled the motor ever so slightly and turned the boat's wheel. We were backing up, and I could see the dock slowly slide away from the port railing as if it were releasing us gently to the sea. With a few extra RPMs, *Surveyor* swung effortlessly 180 degrees away from the dock and floated slowly toward an opening in the harbor. I could see that once we were past that spot, we would be heading into bigger waters. I couldn't hide the smile on my face as Dale navigated a sweeping left turn and headed north.

As the dock and the other big boats that were still moored grew smaller and smaller in the distance, the Alaskan scenery in front of us expanded. So did my gratitude to the Maker of the Seas for the reality that we were actually underway, sailing into my dream.

18

Sailors and Hunters

When *Surveyor* was well out of the harbor, Dale pushed her throttle forward. Even with two decks between the wheelhouse and the engine room, I could hear the big diesel roar with authority. The sustained rumble felt very powerful. The combination of 365 horses and a very strong, nickel-bronze prop easily brought the big vessel to a cruising speed of about nine knots. The weather was picture-perfect as the pointed bow cut the water and created a bubbly white splash on each side of the hull. I looked through the rear windows of the pilothouse and saw that *Surveyor* was leaving a significant mark in the bay that would take a good while to heal. It looked like the wake was a mile long. Awesome!

Except to go below a couple of times to visit the head, refresh my coffee, and grab a granola bar, I didn't leave the pilothouse during the entire six-hour voyage to Chichagof Island. There was something about the Alaskan territory that made me keep looking at it. I was almost afraid to blink for fear of missing something. I tried to imagine how pleased God must have been when He created the majestic bluish mountains, covered them with spruce trees of various green hues, capped them with brilliant white snow, surrounded most of them with deep-blue water, and then painted a bright-blue sky peppered with fluffy gray-and-white clouds. What a masterpiece of living art for us to enjoy!

Surveyor pilothouse

There was another reason I didn't want to go below. Dale was revealing that he wasn't the quiet individual I'd thought. He'd gotten sufficient rest, and his energy and sense of humor were showing as he called everyone topside. He went over the rules to follow while we were on board. The first topic was the head and shower. He said he wanted to start there because those were the two rooms everyone would use and were frequently the most abused places on the boat.

With captain-like sternness and some added tongue-in-cheek content for entertainment value, he gave us his instructions.

- "Always secure the head door after entering so the little red light on the outside comes on. This is to let the rest of us know it's occupied. Otherwise, there'll be bowels locking up due to shock and unwanted overexposure."
- "Turn the exhaust fan on in the head. It exists for an obvious reason. If the air is 'damaged,' flip the switch for the sake of the next guy's respiratory health."
- "Always hold the flushing lever down long enough to completely wash the walls of the commode after doing a 'major' job. The goal is a bowl that is only white after use."
- "Always close the commode lid after using it and correctly

cleansing it. Let there be no fumes escaping from the sewage system holding tank due to an open lid. The smell could be so heavy it could make the boat sink. Well, not really, but everybody might wish it would."

- "Conserve the freshwater as much as possible. For example, don't let the water run while brushing your teeth. If we run out of potable water too soon, the shower will be closed and folks could get gamey. Or worse, we'd run out of water for the coffeepot—a tragedy of inconceivable proportions."
- "In the shower, wet down, turn the water off, and then soap up. Turn the water back on and rinse off. Anyone heard taking a teenager-length shower will be towel whipped."
- "Pick out a spot for your personal towel to hang and dry, and use only your towel during the voyage. Remember where it is and don't make the mistake of grabbing someone else's towel. Nothing is more disgusting than trading skin cells."
- "After showering, use the squeegee hanging on the door. It's there for you to wipe the water beads off the walls. This is for eliminating the potential for smelly mildew and to test to see if everyone is listening."

Dale tutors his new sailors and hunters

I've never enjoyed bathroom and shower instructions so much. Dale's animated mannerisms and choice of images endeared us to him. The tutoring that came next was even more engaging. It was a string of tips about bear hunting. Dale's tone shifted noticeably from humorous to serious.

Dale had plenty to offer as an experienced bear guide. I listened carefully to his insights because if the opportunity presented itself to squeeze the trigger of the .325 while a brownie was in the scope, I didn't want to flub it because I hadn't listened to Captain Adams. Here are a few things I learned at the feet of this master Alaskan bear guide.

- "If we've spotted a bear on the beach and we're going ashore to put the stalk on him, follow me after we get out of the skiff. Watch what I do and do the same. Mainly, if I walk in the water, you walk in the water too, and there's a very good reason for it. It's because the beach is very rocky with lots of loose stones and clamshells that can make clicking and breaking sounds under your boots. Nothing can spook a bear quicker than clicks and snaps. They hear birds calling, tree limbs falling, the splash of the waves, and so on, and that's normal, but the clicking and breaking sounds are not normal, and they can hear it. So if we walk in about a foot or two of water, our sounds will be muffled."
- "I've seen guys jump out of the skiff and go ashore refusing to walk with me through the water because they're afraid they'll fall and get wet. I tell them, 'Hey, when you were a kid you loved messing around in puddles. Now here's your chance to enjoy doing it some more—and with a real benefit!'"
- "If you're following me in the water and it gets waist- or chest-high, you might think it's not a good idea, likely because you'll be afraid you might fall and go under. Keep in mind that you'll be more stable in deeper water than if it's shin-high. Deeper water will stabilize you better. Remember, we're trying to defeat the ears of a bear. Besides, we might have to beeline it through deeper water in order to cut him off or get ahead of him. Instead of going a quarter mile around a cove,

we might be able to get to a set-up spot quicker if we brave the deeper water."

- "When we're walking on beach grass, you'll discover there's a lot of debris mixed in it, like mussel shells, sticks, and especially pop weeds. Pop weed has a bulb that will pop like bubble wrap under your feet when you step on it. Bear can hear the popping. It's hard to avoid it for the most part, but the best thing to do is watch where you step and try your best to not step on the pop weed. In order to eliminate as much of the popping as possible, better yet, step in my steps because I will have already mashed the weed down, snapped the sticks, or popped the bulbs."
- "If there are three of us walking in a line and putting a stalk on a bear, while you're watching where you're stepping try hard to also keep an eye out for my stop signal—my right hand down to my side with my palm facing behind me. We don't want to have the Slinky effect. That's what can happen when I stop, the guy behind me stops a moment later, and finally the last guy stops. If a bear's head is coming up, he *won't* catch me moving, he *might* catch the second guy moving, but he *will* catch the third guy's movement. So don't

Bear anatomy and shot placement clinic

watch the guy in front of you. Watch me. If I signal to stop, I need everyone to stop at the same time, for good reason. If the bear sees the Slinky thing happen, he'll get spooked and take off.

- "As for bullet placement in a bear, you hear people all the time say, 'You gotta break him down. Shoot him in the shoulder and he won't be able to get away.' That's not true!" Dale held up a shoulder blade bone from a brown bear that had a pencil-sized hole in it. "See how wide this bone is? It's impossible to break the shoulder blade. You can poke a hole in it with a bullet like one of my hunters did when he shot this bear, but you're not gonna break it like they say. Besides, a bear can run on three legs as fast as he can with four. His front leg might be wounded so bad that it's spinning like a windmill while he runs, but he'll still run. You gotta hit the bear in the vitals—shoot behind the shoulder. That's your hot spot."
- "An ideal shot distance with a bear is a hundred yards or less. Of course, the ideal position is broadside. But if you want to take a bear that's closer, say thirty or even fifteen yards away because he surprised us, and it appears he's not going to turn broadside, put your crosshairs on his shoulder close to the base of the neck and wait for the right moment to put a bullet in that spot. A big bear's head will swing side to side as he lumbers along. When his head is as far right or left as it will go, and the base of his neck is most visible, shoot at that moment. The only time you'll have to do this is on a short-distance shot because if he's a hundred yards out and facing you as he's coming, you're still waiting and hoping he'll turn broadside. If he's walking toward you at thirty yards or less, it'll likely be because there's no grass for him to stop and eat, which means he's probably not gonna stop and go broadside. Stay calm, if you can, and let me say it again—wait for the swing of the head and go for the open neck."

- "When it comes time to shoot, I'll verbally walk you through it. Be sure to listen to me after the first shot. Keep in mind that a black bear will often run from whatever hits him. He usually won't give you a chance to shoot again where he was standing. A big brown, however, will usually stay and attack whatever he thinks bit him. More often than not, he'll spin in search of his enemy. That reaction will give you a chance to chamber another bullet and get the crosshairs on him. Your next shot will give you a chance for yet another, and so on. Keep in mind that in most cases your first shot will be from a resting position with no movement in the scope. However, once you connect and the bear starts defending himself, the shot placement instantly becomes harder to choose. You'll probably have to raise your gun and shoot off-hand. If that happens, aim for the forward part of the body as best you can and keep shooting until he's down."
- "If it's late in the evening, especially on the last day of the hunt, and the bear is near or facing the heavy timber when you take the first shot, I will likely take a second shot right behind yours just to make sure we don't end up with a wounded bear running into the thick timber. That's a situation that can make for a long night and a potentially dangerous search."

By the time Dale ran through these important pointers, my adrenaline pump was just about worn out. I loved every second of the class, and I took a stack of mental notes as he talked. I prayed I'd be able to remember everything.

As the videographer, Lindsey asked for some tips on filming a stalk and kill. Dale's response was brief but very helpful.

> Just try not to jerk when the gun goes off. Some people just can't keep the camera steady when they hear a loud boom. Of course, a solid rest is the key. If you can set the camera either on a tripod, or a backpack, or even a log or rock, you won't miss the entire shot sequence. I can't tell you how many disappointed hunters I've seen who watch

the playback of a kill and nearly cry when they see nothing but a blurry mess or only the sky immediately after the gun is fired. Just don't jerk!

And one more thing, Lindsey. It might be necessary for you to stay back to capture a stalk and the shot. Two stalkers are much better than three if the ground is really noisy or if the terrain doesn't offer much cover. If I ask you to stay back, rest the camera on something solid and use your zoom feature. The number one priority is getting a bullet in the bear. I know the filming is important, but if the conditions are wrong it has to take second place. Hopefully the two will come together on this hunt.

19

Throttle Down

During the multihour voyage northerly from Sitka, Dale maintained *Surveyor*'s average speed at about eight knots. I had determined to stay wide awake the whole time to enjoy the scenery and the engaging conversation with everyone. However, after about five and half hours down the watery road, the sustained hum of the boat's engine, the lulling sway of *Surveyor*, and the residual effects of the time change caused my eyelids to droop. The voices of my sailing companions and the engine noise faded. Against my will, the back of my head pressed against the window behind where I sat, and I was fast asleep.

I may have been nearing the fourth stage of slumber where total unconsciousness exists (as well as drool) when something happened that caused me to suddenly open my eyes and sit up straight. I'd felt it before when I was with my young kids on an overnight fishing trip in the Gulf of Mexico. The captain of the boat we chartered would leave a fishing hole and head to another, sometimes motoring for ten or fifteen minutes.

While he piloted the boat toward our new destination, we would go to the galley and sit around eating and taking in some fluids. We could hardly hear each other talking over the constant sound of the engine roaring at full bore. Then at a most unexpected moment, the loud throb of the motor would suddenly reduce to a low decibel as the boat slowed and settled in the water.

After a few times of feeling the drastic change, we figured out that it held a very special meaning. The sudden drop in volume and speed meant it was time to fish again. We started anticipating the good feeling it fostered. To this day, it's one of the best memories of our trip. That's why I awoke. I felt *Surveyor*'s voice suddenly change from a roar to a purr, and our forward motion slowed. It told me something exciting could be happening.

Sure enough, when I looked around, we were entering a beautiful cove where the water appeared as smooth as glass. The beach was only two hundred yards to our starboard side as we gradually moved along. Slowly, Dale navigated to within about seventy-five yards of the shore. I could see there were innumerable baseball-sized rocks that made up the beach. The timberline was about fifty yards from the shoreline. The trees on the edge were well lit by the daylight, but immediately behind them was forest that looked as dark as the inside of an abandoned coal mine. It was eerily black.

Surveyor anchored in the cove

As I listened to the exchanges between Dale and Alex, I learned that the cove we'd entered was where they would anchor *Surveyor* for the night. I was captivated by the moment. After fifty years of dreaming and more than a year of planning, fighting worry, anticipating the departure, trudging through five airports, and enduring herds of other travelers—not to mention being a reluctant flyer—I had finally arrived. I settled into the moment just as *Surveyor* settled in the water when Dale pulled the throttle back.

Peace and quiet. What an incredible reward for all the effort. I stepped out of the pilothouse and stood next to the skiff crane so I could look across the railing at the remote Alaskan wilderness. *Surely this will be in heaven—or is this heaven already?*

For a couple of minutes I took in the sound—or the absence of it. So many noises were noticeably missing. No traffic, no trains, no jets overhead, no sirens in the distance. Just quiet—until Alex stepped out on the bow and prepared the anchor for dropping.

Suddenly, *Surveyor* vibrated stem to stern. I instantly recognized the feeling as well as the sound that accompanied it. I'd heard it while working on the USS *Forrestal* during my time in the Navy. It was caused by the anchor chain sliding and bouncing forcefully over the metal roller mounted in the center of the bow point. On the aircraft carrier, the weight of the huge anchor pulled the chain off its storage spool with great ease and speed. The process was more than just the dropping of the anchor, it was an announcement to all aboard that we were going to be in a location for more than a little while. The same was true when *Surveyor*'s chain was released. I was a happy man.

The three-person crew was busy during the first thirty minutes of stopping in the cove. Besides dropping the anchor, Lori got things ready for dinner in the galley while Alex and Dale teamed up to drop the skiffs in the water, where they would stay until our return to Sitka nine days later. It took about twenty minutes for the smaller crafts to be strapped up, hoisted off their bunks, and lowered onto the surface of the cove. I watched the entire process, imagining myself riding in one of them across the wide bay that I could see beyond the cove.

The skiffs were color-coded. One had a red rail and the other a green rail. The aft, middle, and bow seats were molded into the fiberglass hull and unpadded. I had been in boats with hard fiberglass seats and remembered how tough they can be on my relatively unpadded bottom. Thankfully, Dale was aware that some of his hunters suffer from the dreaded "bony butt syndrome," and he had a solution to the problem. I was about to learn what it was when he announced that it was time to board the skiffs with our rifles, motor across the bay, and test fire our weapons.

Dale deploys a skiff

20

Test Firing

On Monday afternoon around five o'clock, the announcement was made that it was time to go ashore across the bay to test fire our guns. It's a standard requirement that every guide I've been with imposes, and for very good reasons. One, to make sure that the scope is still in alignment after a long and sometimes brutal trip through the airline baggage process. Two, and just as important, to ensure that the *hunter* is prepared for the moment of truth by knowing how to fire his weapon.

To get to the beach where we would shoot, we had to ride in the skiffs. It would be my maiden voyage in one of the "twin children" of *Surveyor* but definitely not the last. I joined all the guys at the transom. Dale and the four of us who were guests on the trip were gathered inside the main rail, all wearing our waders, heavy coats, and the life jackets we'd chosen from the boat's equipment rack. I picked out a bright reddish-orange vest because I thought it would be more visible to someone sitting in a search-and-rescue helicopter.

Alex was outside the boat standing on what was essentially the vessel's back porch. It was a ten-foot-wide, four-foot-deep platform where we would board the skiffs. It had four horseshoe-shaped safety rails made of heavy aluminum pipe. There were openings between each section about two feet wide.

Surveyor's back porch

We handed Alex our rifles and the dry packs containing our ammo, and he put them on the skiff floor. At his request, we also passed him a trio of square pads that resembled bases on a baseball diamond. He set them on the bare skiff seats.

Once all the gear was loaded, we were to climb over the rail, descend the ladder that hung on the outside center of the transom, step onto the porch, and then step into one of the skiffs. Even with the generous size of the platform, it was intimidating to look down at it and see the bay just inches beneath the planks. The idea of stepping off *Surveyor* and into a rocking, somewhat unstable small boat put the heebie-jeebies in my head. I definitely didn't want to mess up and fall into the bone-chilling water. The shock to my body would literally take my breath away. I carefully and deliberately stepped across the nonskid planks of the porch.

With everyone in the skiffs safely, Dale and Alex fired up the outboard twenty-five-horsepower Yamaha motors. They started right away, and after about a minute of warm-up, each pilot twisted the throttle on the steering arm, and we were on our way.

All day long I'd been looking down at the Alaskan sea from the vantage point of *Surveyor*'s main deck and pilothouse. Sitting in the skiff felt really strange. Life is extra exciting sitting so close to the water's surface and knowing that the only thing between me and certain death was about two inches of fiberglass. Turning around to see that *Surveyor* was getting farther away with each passing second made the ride even more intense.

Within a half-minute, we were 500 yards from the big boat with at least a ten-minute ride ahead to the shore, where we'd fire our guns. I felt exhilarated, primitive, manly, and grateful to be where I was.

Once we were outside the cove where there was more wind, the surface of the water changed from calm to choppy. The ride also changed, and that's when I learned how valuable the square seat pads were. And it wasn't just because they doubled as flotation devices. They also were there to protect our backsides.

When we were cruising at top speed across the water, the hull slightly bounced on the whitecaps and created a manageable vibration. Every once in a while, however, a set of bigger waves would collide with the hull and result in repeated quick rises and sudden falls. My body was bounced into the air, momentarily suspended, and then dropped down. By the time I came down, the hull was coming up again. The butt beating was a challenge. Without the pad, my tailbone might have knocked a hole in the hull seat. How thankful my bony backside was for the heavy pad.

Around five forty-five that evening, Dale and Alex slowed the Yamaha motors as we neared the beach. When we were about fifty yards from the shoreline, they cut the motors and drifted forward another twenty-five yards. Then they both got out of the skiffs and held them still in the knee-deep water.

Like we'd been told, the shore was much too rocky for the fiberglass hulls. The guides dropped bell-type anchors into the water and proceeded to the beach while unspooling a long, yellow mooring rope. After tying them to large rocks half the size of Volkswagens, our guides instructed us to grab our gear, exit the skiffs, and come ashore.

It was exciting to step out for the first time onto an Alaska beach. I felt the pressure of the water surround my legs, and even through my waders and long johns I could tell the water was very cold. Walking on the rocks that slid around under my waders wasn't easy. It took only a few steps to figure out that it was a little like walking a tightrope. I could see how deeper water would be more stabilizing, as Dale had mentioned. Though it was a little tricky to get to the beach without falling, it felt good to get there and still be dry under the waders.

Dale went back to the skiff he'd been in and got a large piece of cardboard with a solid black circle about three inches in diameter in the center. He walked about sixty yards down the beach and leaned it against a rock that stood about four feet tall. I had a feeling he'd been at this range many times before.

This better be good!

"Load 'em up, boys!" Dale gave the order when he was about ten yards from us. There was a look in his eye that seemed to say, "This better be good!"

I felt the pressure. In a matter of minutes I would be pulling the trigger on the .325 with a gallery of hunters standing behind me. If I didn't poke a hole in the cardboard at least a couple of inches from the black dot, I would cease to be a hunter and become a question mark in the minds of the legendary Dale Adams and his worthy protégé. At that moment, I felt as if I were about to tee off on the first hole of a golf tournament with Bubba and Tom Watson watching me.

To break the tension, I thought about repeating something I said to the fellow who had guided my son, Nathan, and me on our first elk hunt out West several years earlier. He too required us to fire our weapons before we headed out to hunt. As we got into his truck to go to the range, he asked, "Do you have your ammo with you?"

I answered, "I just brought one bullet."

"What?" He looked at me thinking I was serious. "You brought only one bullet? Seriously?"

With a straight face I said, "Well, I'm only allowed one elk."

There was a blank stare on his face for about three seconds, and then it dawned on him that I was joking. He laughed, and I was relieved.

I decided not to try the "one bullet" joke with Dale and Alex, who appeared all business as they waited for me to take a shot. It was time to face the music, so I put in my soft-rubber ear protectors and loaded the clip with four bullets. As I did, Jason announced he was ready to shoot. I was so glad he went first, but then I thought, *What if he centers his shot in the black dot? How could I follow that?*

Laying across a three-foot-tall rock, my fellow hunter squeezed the trigger. Rock dust flew behind the cardboard. Dale used his binoculars and said, "Good shot! Two inches left of center. You're good."

It was my turn. My knees felt weak and pained by the jagged stones beneath them as I knelt at the same rock Jason had used. I rested the gun on a beanbag that was sitting on the dome of the rock and found the cardboard in my scope. I forced myself to focus on the target and not think about the crowd watching my performance. It was good

Man talk

practice for facing a bear. In fact, I tried to imagine that the cardboard was a big brown standing there broadside.

"Y'all ready?"

Their voices were muffled by my ear protection as they gave me the vocal go-ahead.

I gave the warning, "Fire in the hole," and gently pulled the trigger.

Suddenly the gun jolted me backward. Before the echo of the blast died, I had my eye back on the scope to see if I could tell where the bullet hit. As I was about to say it, Dale said, "Two inches right of center. That's good!"

I stood up, turned around, and didn't see anyone looking worried. The tee shot was in the fairway. As Dale went to get the target I thought, *If I get to pull the trigger again here in Alaska, it won't be at cardboard.* Chills!

21

The Bear Song

There was still plenty of daylight remaining after the test firing, and that's when I heard a short song that made my soul rejoice. Dale went to retrieve the target, and on his way back to the group he folded it up while singing, "Big brown bear, big brown bear, let's go find a big brown bear!" It was a song he'd composed years earlier and loved to perform for his hunters. The words were music to my ears.

With those lyrics and the fun melody, I knew it was official. I had passed the test firing, and my guide was happy. I didn't know him all that well, but I could sense that if he didn't feel confident our rifles had survived the nearly 3000-mile, scope-jarring journey, and if he didn't think we were capable and safe firearm handlers who were ready for an encounter with a brownie, he wouldn't have sung those glorious words. There was too much at stake—our safety and his reputation.

My heart was racing as we walked back into the water, placed our gear in the two waiting skiffs, climbed in, and took our seats on the precious shock-absorbing pads. The engines came to life, and twenty seconds later we were motoring in opposite directions in parties of three. Dale, Lindsey, and I were in the green-railed skiff while our host, Jason, and Alex were in the red-railed version. Our two guides had apparently discussed where we'd hunt for the evening. They pointed the skiff bows toward those spots and turned the throttles to full speed ahead.

The temperature while standing on the beach just minutes earlier was a balmy forty degrees. When the skiff was at full bore, the wind chill felt like twenty. I started zipping up my big coat and noticed my hands weren't steady. What was wrong? My entire body wanted to shake. I silently said, *Dude, it's not that cold. Man up!* Then it hit me.

I was having the same reaction to the cold Alaska wind that I had experienced on more than one occasion in Tennessee while deer hunting on chilly, early fall mornings. It's a phenomena that can happen when even a moderately cool temperature interacts with the presence of a mature buck. The collision of the two forces can cause an extreme rush of adrenaline to course through my veins. My nerve endings react like the tail end of an angry rattlesnake. In this case, I hadn't even seen a bear yet and I was super excited. I was relieved to know I wasn't experiencing a cardiac episode.

After about twenty-five minutes of scooting and bouncing across the bay at fifteen knots, Dale throttled back the outboard motor, and the skiff bow settled gently into the water. As noted earlier, I love that feeling. Something was up. The motor was still running, gently vibrating the hull.

Sitting in the center bench, I turned to see what Dale was doing and to check out the expression on his face. I think I'm pretty good at reading a hunter's facial signs. I've seen enough wide-eyed looks on friends' faces to recognize when they see something that has them at full alert. I wanted to determine if that look was on Dale's face, but I couldn't see it. When I looked back, he was standing with his entire face covered by his gloved hands and a pair of binoculars that were not just an average, run-of-the-mill pair like mine.

When I saw what he was holding, I was embarrassed to take my pair out of my daypack. Compared to Dale's substantial, fat, olive-green, ten-inch binocs with front lenses that looked as big as the bottom of a mayonnaise jar, mine looked like opera glasses on a stick that a princess would use in a theater balcony.

I didn't say anything as my guide balanced himself in the slightly swaying skiff and glassed the beach that was at least a thousand yards away. After about a minute, he sat back down and appeared pensive. I was just about to ask him the hunter's all-time favorite question: "See anything?" The words were forming on my lips when he beat me to the verbal punch. His voice was very subdued as he spoke in a deliberate whisper.

"By the way, guys, one thing I forgot to tell you. When the motor is rumbling, even at a low volume, it's normal to want to raise your voice to be heard over it. We have to avoid that mistake because as you know, water can carry your vocals like a microphone through a sound system. It's one of nature's strange features—and a bear is not deaf. So when you can, use hand signals. If I can't hear what you're saying and you need me to hear it, crawl back here and whisper in my ear. Of course, if the engine is off and everything is quiet, we can hear whispering."

Lindsey and I didn't have to hear that tip again. We were obedient students and willing followers. From that moment on, while on the water our communication was kept to pointing, nodding heads, and silently forming words in an exaggerated way so that our lips could be read.

Dale poured the fuel to the motor again and went closer to shore. As we rounded a point that jutted out into the bay, he throttled down and slowly motored the skiff into a huge cove that wasn't long and deep like an inlet. Instead, it was shaped like a giant "C."

About 500 yards in, he pointed the bow of the skiff toward the beach, turned the motor off, and floated to within twenty yards of the rocky shore. Dale got out, dropped the anchor in the thigh-deep water, and whispered, "Let's go!" He got his rifle and the mooring rope spool, I got my weapon, Lindsey grabbed our dry packs, and the three of us headed to the beach. Dale unspooled about seventy-five feet of mooring rope and tied it to an old, heavy log that had washed ashore. Then we walked in a line like soldiers to another gigantic log that had washed up and was lying nearly perpendicular to the waterline about a hundred yards down the beach.

Dale quietly said, "Let's sit here for the rest of the evening." He pointed to the deepest part of the cove and added, "That far meadow has hosted a lot of bears. There are some grasses in it they really like. From time to time they'll come off the mountain on the far side of this cove, feed in that meadow, and then work their way around to where we're sitting."

For the next two hours we frequently glassed the meadow, looked right and left down the beach as well as behind us, and kept our conversation to a whisper. As we talked, Dale added another bear-hunting tip to our war chest of wise tactics.

"Spotting a bear is *not* that easy." He pointed again to the deepest part of the massive cove and said, "That far meadow is farther away than it appears. It's at least a quarter of a mile over there, and even a big bear at that distance will be hardly more than a dark spot to the naked eye. It'll look like a dot that's slowly moving. If you see a dark spot, don't trust your eyes alone. Stop, put your binocs on it, and watch it for a few seconds. If it moves, bingo! You're probably seeing a bear. It could be a deer in the shadows, so keep your eyes on it until you know for sure what it is. The moment you think you see something moving, be sure to tell me. I'll help you figure out if you're seeing a bear or a tree stump. And if it's a bear, I'll help you figure out if it's a boy or a girl."

First evening hunt for "big brown bear"

Sitting on an Alaskan beach, frequently adjusting our bottoms to endure the uneven surface of the rocky shore, conversing about everything from bear habits to politics, watching for moving black, furry-looking dots…it was much more fun than grown men should be allowed to have. The two hours passed much too quickly. As the sun was falling behind the mountains in the west, Dale gathered his gear and said, "Suppertime, boys! Let's go to the house."

On the way back to the skiff, I started whisper-singing in advance of the next day's hunt, "Big brown bear, big brown bear, let's go find a big brown bear." Lindsey joined in. A smile came to Dale's face as he heard his song being covered by a couple of Nashville musicians.

22

What's Not for Dinner?

As we motored toward *Surveyor* in the darkness, we wouldn't know until we all got back that this first hunt had ended with no shots fired. Though getting a bear was the goal, doing it quickly would have meant being finished with the hunt for whoever filled his tag. Besides, we weren't thinking about bear at nine o'clock at night. We had our minds on food.

Much to our delight, when we boarded the big boat we found that Lori had dinner just about ready. She knew from experience that all of us would be hungry enough to eat a moose down to the hoof. The aroma of her cooking made us salivate. Everything smelled so good that I was inspired to sing my rewrite of the chorus of an old gospel song as we gathered around the table: "When the rolls are served up yonder, I'll be there!"

Regarding the food aboard the boat, it was unbelievably tasty and consistently plentiful. Whether we were having chicken and rice, Mexican fare, Italian, or hearty country-style dishes, it was invariably delicious. I could feel my pants shrinking from the weight gain as the week progressed. Try as I might, I couldn't seem to find the willpower to stop when my full switch flipped. The food was just too tasty.

In regard to the self-stuffing that was happening at the table, I recall an especially funny moment that happened toward the end of our first evening's dinner. I was so full that I began to moan, begging someone to put duct tape over my mouth or staple my lips shut. Dale sat around the corner of the table from me. He listened to my groaning, gave me a deadly serious look, and spoke as if he were coaching me in my attempt to set the world record for how much food one man could hold. He tilted his head sideways, reached out and put his left hand on my shoulder, and said, "Don't give up, man. You gotta push through. Just keep pushin'. Come on, you gotta push through."

It was dangerous for me to laugh at that moment. The pressure on my midsection could have made me explode. But laugh I did until it hurt. Everyone else laughed too because they were just as stuffed as I was. From that moment on, we often repeated, "Gotta just push through." It always brought a laugh, especially at the dining table.

Of all the food consumed aboard the vessel, the most anticipated was fresh seafood. It wasn't purchased or shipped in. Instead, we caught it in the water surrounding our floating hotel.

You gotta push through

Our mornings didn't include hunting because bears feed through the night and bed down during the day. They don't typically move in the early hours. A few did, but not many. In fact there was only one morning hunt. Other than that, we did what Dale called "matinee hunting." After lunch, we'd head out on the skiffs and hunt until dark, which came around eight o'clock. That schedule allowed us to use the mornings to drop pots—wire, cage-like, baited traps—in the water to catch shrimp and crab. We also got to fish with rod and reel from the skiffs.

Digging for dinner...clams anyone?

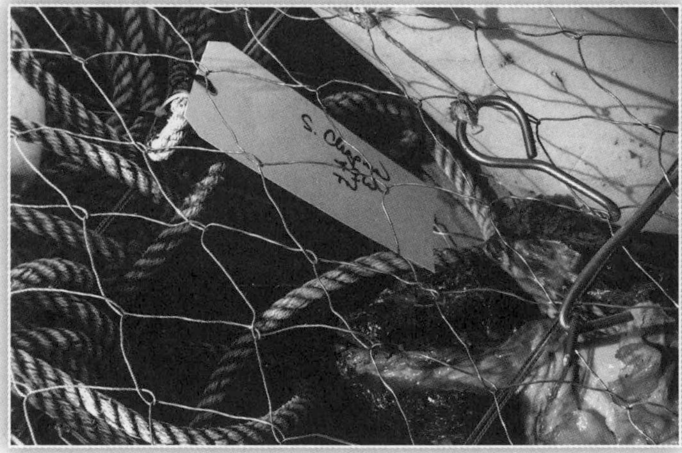

The winning pot...sometimes!

Each pot was marked with a colored, ball-shaped buoy attached to the retrieving line. Each one was also tagged with the name of one of the group members to create some fun competition to see who brought in the biggest catch.

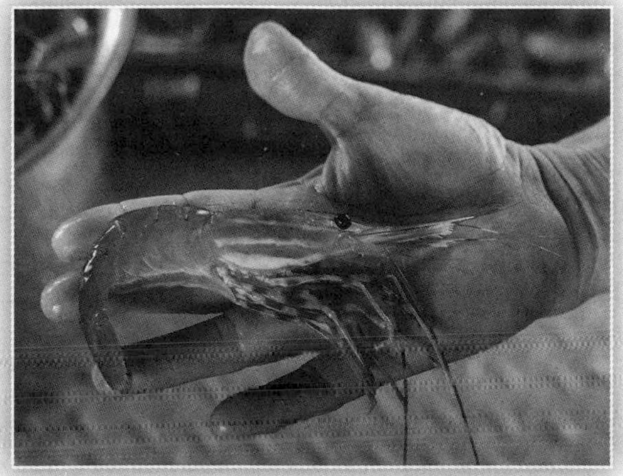

Are you gonna eat that? Oh yeah!

As a team, we loaded the pots into the skiffs and motored to spots that had a good reputation for yielding a catch. The next morning, we'd return to the buoys and pull them to the surface. It was always fun (and appetizing!) to see how full they were with live seafood. Some were so heavy it was hard to get them into the boat. Some were nearly empty, and we always jokingly blamed the light catch on the one whose name was on the buoy.

We'd take the catch back to the boat, where the shrimp would be poured onto a ten-foot, square, knee-high plate that was actually the cover for the boat's storage bay. Hundreds of wriggling shrimp would spread out in all directions, and everyone would gather around to prepare them for cooking by snapping their heads off and putting them in a huge pot of freshwater. They would be boiled and put away for later uses, which included frying, making cheese-and-shrimp breakfast sandwiches, topping salads, tossing into gumbo, and more.

The crabs required a tutorial for those of us who were inexperienced with the special handling they required. The key was to avoid the claws that could clamp down on a finger hard enough to nearly sever the digit and test the victim's control over his tongue. Once the crabs were removed from the cage, they were dropped into a live well for later consumption. It was strange to look into the tank and see a lot of active creatures resembling Tennessee crawdads on steroids.

Whether the meals included shrimp or crab or other seafood, Lori's entrees and side dishes were phenomenal. And then there were the desserts—especially the candied apples, which proved I'd lost all self-control. The coffee was always good, hot, and flowing, especially at dessert time. After a few of the "gotta just push through" experiences, the question I started asking wasn't, "What's for dinner?" It was, "What's *not* for dinner?" We were sure roughing it.

Lori's incredible candied apple

23

A Day "Two" Remember, Part 1

Lori's awesome, belly-busting dinner on Monday evening and the great conversation afterward was quite a finale. The day began with an early wake-up call at the hotel and continued with a glorious, sun-blessed, six-hour voyage into the endless, shore-lined remotes of the Last Frontier. Then came the spine-challenging skiff ride to the beach, where my nerves and my credibility as a shooter were tested, followed by my very first hunt on Alaskan soil for a mighty brown boar. Whew!

The post-meal fellowship was sweet, but eventually the droop-eye set in on everyone. We dispersed to our assigned cabins. My nearly six-and-a-half-decade-old body was begging for rest and didn't protest the decision to retire, but my mind did. I wasn't sure if I'd ever be able to stop the mental highlight reel that kept replaying all the incredible things that had happened that day. It helped to talk to Lindsey, but he faded faster than I did. I was alone in the dark with my thoughts.

This boat's not swaying, so it must be mighty calm out there. Matinee hunting...hmmm...not a bad thing since it means we don't have to get up every day before daylight. I can live with that. Tennessee sure is a long way from this cove. There's no cell service here...gotta try to check in with that satellite phone Dale mentioned...sure hope Annie and the family are doing well and not worried about me. God, bless them every one. And, God, especially be with my dad tonight. Touch him...it's a long way to West Virginia, but Your hand can reach him.

The next thought I had was about seven hours later. *I wonder if the red light is on outside the head door! Gotta go—and now.*

As I climbed out of the bunk, I had another flashback of being on the aircraft carrier. Back then I had to be very careful when I dismounted from the top bunk to not step on the face or arm or any other part of a fellow sailor in the bottom bunk—and to avoid waking him up. I managed to not rouse Lindsey as I dropped to the floor and went to the head. The light was off—thankfully.

Monster creature, starboard side!

It appeared that I was the first one up on that Tuesday morning. I took the opportunity to tiptoe up to the pilothouse and check out the cove in the early light. What a view! The water was so flat that it looked like I could walk on it to the beach. A few seagulls were busy on some big rocks in the distance, and some big black birds that looked like ravens were enjoying the tops of the spruces that lined the shore. I picked up a pair of binoculars and scanned the area…and then I saw it—*whoa!*

About 300 yards off the port side of *Surveyor*, the motionless surface of the water suddenly rose about eight feet and then gently opened to reveal a large, rounded section of a huge, dark and shiny sea creature. It was a humpback whale! What a good-morning welcome to Alaska!

The appearance lasted only a couple of seconds, but I knew the memory of it would last for the rest of my life.

As I processed the grand privilege of seeing such an incredible sight live and in color, I saw a couple more humpbacks in the area. A thought hit me that was a bit disconcerting. *What if a skiff was at the very spot where a whale's back rose out of the water? Yikes! It would surely capsize the boat and dump whoever was in it into the frigid bay. What then? What if I was in the skiff?* I swallowed hard. I decided at that very moment to not let the possibility stop me from climbing into the small craft and doing what I had come to Alaska to do. Besides, there is no grace for borrowed sorrow.

Putting the worst-case, skiff-dumping scenario aside, I spent another ten minutes watching for a few more appearances of the leviathans. They obliged and provided quite a show that included some spouts from their blowholes. It was amazing to watch the blast of warm, misty air shoot straight up fifteen or twenty feet, turn into a huge teardrop shape, linger a few seconds, and then fade to nothing. After seeing a half dozen or so of the unique sprays and observing how they would appear, stay for a moment, and then go away, I thought of a well-known verse in the Bible that says, "You are just a vapor that appears for a little while and then vanishes away" (James 4:14). Like a whale's spray, we come, we hang around for just a little while, and then we disappear.

Momentary sighting, lifetime memory

In the middle of pondering the brevity of life, I heard footsteps coming up the stairs leading to the pilothouse. It was Lindsey—with coffee. As he looked out the windows, he made a full 360-degree spin on his heels. He could only say one word to describe the scenery: "Wow!"

I told him about the whale activity, and for twenty minutes we had fun pointing to the places where the water would heave upward and seemingly give birth to a whale's back or to where a spout would happen.

"There!"

"Over there!"

"Check it out over here!"

I opened one of the sliding windows in the pilothouse and leaned out to listen for the sound of the blow. It was faint, but I could hear it.

We are but a vapor...

Lindsey's camera shutter was clicking like someone was doing Morse code, and the 64GB smart card in my video camera was drinking in the whale action. I thought, *Sure wish Annie could see this live and in color too*. Not five seconds later, Lindsey said, "Sure wish Susan could see this." I made him aware that we were sharing a moment of wifely mush. We were still smiling about it when the call came from below deck that breakfast was served.

Amazed that we were actually hungry after the volume of food we'd put away the evening before, we joined our adventure mates in the galley. After thanks was given, the pancakes started flying like playing cards around the table. Within fifteen minutes, we were all saying, "Gotta just push through" to each other and declaring we wouldn't eat again until the next day, which, of course, wasn't true.

We spent the morning gathering, emptying, and re-baiting the shrimp and crab pots. We loaded them into the skiffs and dropped them in the water not too far from *Surveyor*. Lunchtime came quickly, and we ate again. Then it was time to put on our waders, water boots, and life jackets; grab our guns and dry packs; and head out for our first full-length, matinee hunt.

Dale took Lindsey and me in one skiff; Alex took Jason and our host in the other. We motored away at three in the afternoon going in different directions. All of us were hopeful that at least one of the parties would return in the evening and do the traditional, full-speed flyby around *Surveyor* in the skiff. To Lori and anyone else on board, it would mean that a bear was down.

24

A Day "Two" Remember, Part 2

As we left *Surveyor* for the evening hunt on Tuesday, Dale waited until we were about twenty-five yards out and then brought the skiff up to full speed. It slid smoothly across the calm water inside the deep cove. Just before we entered the open water of the bay, I turned around, looked back at the big boat, and studied the distance we'd gone from her. Suddenly some chilling questions crossed my mind. *Isn't this about where we saw the whales this morning? Where are they now? Are they still around?*

I turned forward and looked at Lindsey, who was sitting in the bow seat facing the back of the skiff. Using hand signals, I tried to convey

Heading out for the evening hunt

my thoughts. He understood that I was referring to the whales we'd seen. Then I did the nails-in-the-teeth sign that said, "Nervous!" He just pursed his lips and shook his head as if to say, "It ain't gonna happen, dude." Thankfully, he was right.

Glassing from the rocks

Dale's plan was to check out some coves and inlets, staying away from shore far enough to avoid spooking a bear that might be moving along the beach yet close enough to be able to determine its sex and size using binoculars. After motoring around for a couple of hours and pausing to observe large sections of shoreline, we stopped and went ashore for about forty-five minutes on a small island. It was made up mostly of jagged, sharp-edged volcanic rock. Walking and climbing on it was risky to our bodies and our waders, but we managed to get to a high spot where we could see at least a couple of miles up and down the straight line of beach.

Not spotting any bear activity, we left the little island and motored slowly, perpendicular to the shoreline. At one point Dale turned the steering arm of the skiff's motor and pointed the bow toward a beach that was nearly half a mile away.

While our guide focused on that spot with his highly effective binoculars, Lindsey and I glassed the beaches in opposite directions. We had the area well covered as each of us slowly scanned the shoreline. Every dark spot was guilty of being a bear until proven innocent. Then we heard Dale sort of grunt. To me, he sounded excited. Five seconds later, he said some words that a smart guide would say only if he was sure he was right.

"Okay, guys, I think we have something here."

"I think we have something here."

Lindsey and I lowered our glasses to see where Dale's binoculars were pointed. We immediately shifted in our seats to check the section of the shoreline he was watching.

"I'm looking at a bear. It's hard to see right now 'cause it's in some shadows, but to find him, look straight ahead for a large whitish log on the shoreline that's halfway in the water. When you find it, go to the left. There's a light-brown, washed-up log lying diagonally on the shore. He's behind it now in some brush. Keep your glasses on that spot, and if he comes back out of the shadows you'll see him."

There was no way I could have joined in the search with the opera glasses I'd brought from home. However, our host had felt sorry for me and insisted I use his very nice pair that was close to Dale's in quality.

The magnification was astounding. As I searched the area Dale pointed out, I suddenly saw a black dot moving along the beach.

"I see it!" With the boat motor off, the high pitch of my whisper easily told Dale and Lindsey how pumped I was. Then Lindsey saw it.

Even while sitting with my elbows resting on my knees, it wasn't easy to keep the glasses steady on the dot as the skiff swayed in the waves. I wondered how Dale managed to do it while standing. Then I remembered how long he'd been guiding and realized that of course he knew how to work around the rocking skiff problem. And I'm glad he did because he was able to feed us information we wouldn't have gotten otherwise.

"It's a male bear—a boar—for sure, and he's moving right to left. I think we ought to slowly motor in and get a better view." Lindsey and I dropped our glasses and exchanged big smiles and "woo-hoo" looks.

The skiff motor started easily, and Dale accelerated slightly to keep the noise to a minimum. Ten minutes later we finally got close enough for him to glass the bear again. He whispered an announcement that made me shiver.

"He's definitely a big bear. I think we should go ashore ahead of him, set up, and see if he walks to us."

He got no resistance from Lindsey and me as we tried to find the bear again in our binoculars while the boat rose and fell on the slightly choppy water. I wasn't able to find him, so I gave up the search and put my trust in my guide's eyes. I used the time to rehearse what to do if a shot was in my near future.

Dale set his course well left of the bear and headed toward an outcropping of rocks that was at least a quarter of a mile from our position. Unable to move along more than two or three miles per hour to keep the sound of the motor to a minimum, it took several minutes to get to our destination. Steering to the left of the fifteen-foot tall, domed-shaped rocks, Dale looked for a place to tie up the skiff beside them.

There was only one place to get close enough, drop an anchor, and safely climb out of the boat onto the rocks. Concerned that the sea and tide movement would make the hull of the skiff bang against the hard wall of stone and make unwanted noise, Dale looked for a way to keep it from happening. Being a master of makeshift that a guide is required to be, he used the mooring rope and wrapped it around the top of a smaller rock and pulled the boat in tight.

"Guys, we need to hurry, but be careful. These rocks can be slippery. Make sure of your footing and follow behind me. The bear is somewhere down the beach on the other side of this outcropping. We don't know how much farther he fed toward us while we were getting to shore, so when we get to the top of these rocks we have to move slowly and be as quiet as we can."

Things were getting serious.

Dale wore his backpack. He and I had our rifles shouldered with slings. Lindsey carried the video camera in his right hand, and his dry-pack, which contained his still camera, was strapped on his shoulder. His climb was a little tougher with only one free hand to balance himself, but we both managed to keep up with our guide, who climbed as confidently as a mountain goat.

Reaching the top of the rocks, Lindsey and I hung back as Dale carefully bellied to the crest and peeked over with his binoculars. Feeling sure we had reached the set-up spot before the bear did, he signaled us to join him.

Other large, rounded rocks of slightly different heights surrounded the big rock we had climbed. There were no deep separations, which allowed us to step down into the shallow valleys and climb up on the next dome. I followed Dale and Lindsey followed me as we headed toward a formation in the rocks that looked like it could be a place to conceal our bodies and provide a rifle rest.

As our threesome was moving across the rocks, Dale and I suddenly heard the distinct sound of a rubber boot slipping on stone and then a painful, barely controlled but sufficiently subdued grunt of a man who was falling. I turned to see a video camera held high to keep it from slamming onto the unfriendly rocks. Lindsey was down—but only momentarily.

As my Tennessee buddy rolled his body over to continue to our set-up spot he whispered, "So sorry about that."

I whispered, "Dude, are you okay?"

"Yes, and so is the camera. Right now that's all that matters!"

In response to the noise of the fall, Dale looked down the beach to see if there might be a bear that heard the commotion and was running away. There was no sign of an escaping beast, so he turned and said something that went down in our hunting history. Smiling, our guide said, "From now on, when someone slips and falls I can say, 'He did a Lindsey!'"

It was not the memory my buddy wanted to leave in Alaska or with one of the state's legendary guides, but he appreciated the humor. We were all grateful, especially Lindsey, that we weren't heading back to the skiff to rush a broken bone or cracked skull back to *Surveyor* and then on to the Sitka hospital by floatplane. God's grace was great and most welcome.

With his backpack off, Dale crouched down in one of the crevices of the rock and was well hidden as he faced the shoreline. The only parts of him visible to a bear were his shoulders and head. I wanted to do the same, but the narrow crevice I was in wouldn't allow me to position my knees forward like Dale had done. Instead, I had to sit a little sideways. I searched the crevice for even a hint of ledge and found that the only seat I could find to rest my bottom on was a sharp shelf that was only three inches wide and six inches long. When I lowered my body onto it, it bit into my right butt cheek. The only thing that helped me ignore the pain was thinking that a bear might be headed our way.

Dale lifted his backpack onto the rock for me to use as a rest for the .325. It worked great. Then he assessed our waiting time. "How long we have to wait depends on how much browsing the bear does along the way. It could be a few minutes or it could be a couple of hours before he gets to us…if he does at all." That last part with the "if" sounded like a wise caveat that a seasoned guide would add since the only thing predictable about hunting is that it's so unpredictable. Dale's professionalism was showing.

When I heard "a couple of hours," I instantly became aware of the pain in my derriere. How could I endure that much time sitting on just a narrow stony ledge that felt like a razor blade? I immediately made a decision to grimace and bear it. I wasn't about to let a temporary pain in my rumpus ruin a nearly 3000-mile trip of a lifetime.

The bear wasn't in sight, so Dale took the opportunity to tutor me on the habits of the animal and how the hunt might play out. "If he didn't go back up into the timber, most likely he's still feeding on beach grasses as he comes this way. There may be a few small meadows that he'll check out. That's why it might take more time than expected. If there's nothing for him to eat, he'll keep coming. We're set up at a spot he's probably been to many times. He knows the area."

The section of shoreline we were monitoring was about 175 yards long. From the water's edge to the start of vegetation was about 30 yards. The open beach was made up of nothing but gravel and a few small logs. Included in the natural debris was an old car tire that the tide had pushed all the way to the grass line. Dale pointed to the tire and said, "If the bear comes down the beach, wait till he gets to that old tire. It's within a hundred yards of us. We don't want to shoot beyond that distance. We need a good, sure hit that will keep him out of the timber."

Setting up and listening to Dale

Every word Dale had said since we heard, "Okay, guys, I think we have something here," while in the skiff made my hair stand up. I felt confident that we were in the middle of something major going down.

I fought to keep my composure and occupied the moment by testing how the .325 was resting on Dale's backpack. Again, I mentally rehearsed the shot routine. Dale whispered that he might take a shot right after my first, and I was very agreeable to the idea. He also comforted me with a reminder that once I fired shot number one, he would start coaching me through any following shots I might take. Even though we were in the midst of a possible encounter with a brown bear, I was hearing his advice as distant echoes of a life's work I never got to do. He was the big-game guide I never was. My respect for him grew with every passing minute—and so did my envy.

All along the backside of the beach we were watching, next to a big wall of spruce, was a stand of shorter, leafy trees that extended toward the water's edge about ten yards. The foliage-laden limbs started about chest-high off the ground and created what appeared to be a tunnel-like passage that an animal could use to get around the sizable heap of loose rocks that were piled at the far end of the open beach. It was dark under the trees. As I kept my eyes on that particular area, I imagined a bear coming out of the shadows into the light. After another minute of staring, I looked away and started readjusting my bottom on my "razor seat."

Twenty seconds later, I felt a quick double tap on the right side of my back. It was Dale. He whispered loudly enough so Lindsey could also hear. "Guys, don't move and don't say a word!"

25

A Day "Two" Remember, Part 3

Instantly I stopped repositioning my behind on the narrow, sharp, rock ledge. I'd hunted long enough to know that if someone alerted me that an animal was in view and I needed to move to see it, I had to turn my head like a shadow on a sundial to not give my presence away.

With my eyes as far right in their sockets as they would go, I started turning my head. It took only a couple of inches before I could see the huge bear coming out of the dark area under the trees just as I'd imagined. In that moment, I couldn't have recalled my name, where I was born, or where I lived. My mind was swirling with excitement, and I had to force myself to think clearly.

Lindsey found the boar in the video camera and held steady as it fed on the vegetation. When the bear's gaze went to the ground to feed, I took the chance to turn my head fully in its direction and lowered my eye to look through the scope on the rifle. In that moment, if someone would have asked me how it felt to see a live bear in my scope instead of the one I'd been imagining for so long, I would have been at a complete loss for words.

At that point, I had no idea whether the big boar would leave the grassy spot he was nosing and continue down the beach toward us. I wondered, *Will he make it as far as the washed-up tire? Will he wind us and run? Will he simply decide his belly is full and wander out of sight into*

There he is!

the dense timber? His unhurried lingering made the seconds pass like hours.

Dale whispered, "If he leaves that patch of grass and gets on the open beach in the gravel, he'll come closer. Other than the deeper grass on his right at the topside of the beach, there's nothing for him to eat until he gets behind us."

Then things turned in our favor.

The bear continued our way, but he stayed up high, near the edge of the thick grass. He stopped occasionally to look around for something edible. I had him in my scope starting at the 150-yard mark and raised my head to watch him with my naked eye a few times. I desperately wanted to take in the raw, unmagnified sight of such a mountainous creature. He looked heavy up close in the scope, but even outside the lenses he was massive. As he slowly lumbered along, his unusually wide head swung side-to-side just as Dale had described. I could see what he meant when he explained how a last-resort, straight-on shot could be effective.

When we first spotted the bear, he was facing the bay. We could see a triangular, hand-size tear in his hide on his upper right hip. It looked like it may have been a battle scar that had healed. When he started down the beach, his left hip was visible, and the hair was perfectly thick and dark. His skull appeared as wide as Dale's broad shoulders. I could see the telltale hump on the back of his neck that is unique to the male bear. It looked just like what I saw when I watched the *Take a Second Look* film that out-of-state hunters are required to watch as part of the brown bear tag application. He was definitely a taker boar!

"He's coming in. Get ready!"

When he was about ten yards from the old tire, I put my eye back to the scope. It was obvious that he was going to walk within Dale's preferred range of a hundred yards or less. A lot of hunters talk about how their hearts wildly race when the moment of truth arrives, but I honestly couldn't feel mine beating. I think it had paused. I didn't feel anything except the trigger under my finger. Then I remembered an incredibly important step that I hadn't yet taken. The safety was still on!

Fighting to remember where it was, I finally found the flat, ribbed slider behind the bolt. Using my thumb, I pushed it forward to the off position and rested my index finger on the trigger guard. By then, the bear was within five yards of the half-buried tire. He was coming in, but there was an angle problem.

He was to my left, and if he kept walking straight ahead, the shot angle would be like he was at ten o'clock in front of me...but on the other side of a two-lane highway. Not good. And if he kept going, he didn't have to walk far to disappear behind the even bigger rocks in the outcropping that were off my left shoulder. If that happened I'd have to move my upper body and gun around to take an off-hand shot. I was sure the movement and noise would spook him because of how close he'd be. The only hope left was that he would turn broadside, preferably somewhere close to the old tire.

Ten seconds later, the brown nearly stepped on the tire, stopped, put his nose to it for a second, and then looked up and around. For just a brief moment he looked in our direction, and I could see his dark eyes through the scope. It was sobering to think that the incredibly strong body behind those eyes was not in a movie, not in a picture, not in my fantasy. He was standing there at a distance he could easily close within seconds if he wanted to.

Though we were basically safe where we sat on the rocks, it was still a test of my willingness to wait for a sure shot. It was as if all the potential dangers involved with bear hunting and the dread of things going wrong were funneling into my emotions. I had to shake my thoughts to resist shooting. I fought to regain full focus on the crosshairs that I had placed behind the bear's shoulder. The angle was still not good, but patience and waiting paid off.

Chilling stare

For a reason known only to the bear and the One who made it, the boar took a step to the right and then another. He paused and looked around. A couple more short steps slightly to the right, and he'd be totally broadside. Like a laser, I stared at his left shoulder through the center of the crosshairs.

Suddenly, everything necessary to make my dream come true

gathered in one dime-sized spot on the planet. I don't remember pulling the trigger, but when the firing pin slammed on the bullet primer, the explosion made the world spin, including the bear. He was fighting against whatever had bit him, just as Dale said he would.

Fully broadside...it's time!

I didn't hear Dale's shot. All I heard was him saying, "Hit him again!"

Oh, that's right! I need to shoot again!

I was embarrassed that I'd let the excitement of my first shot consume me so completely that I delayed jacking another shell into the chamber. I blamed it on Alaska-induced insanity. As fast as I could work the bolt, I slid another bullet in, found the circling bear in the scope, and tried hard to quickly find his chest. As his vitals passed by the crosshairs, I pulled the trigger again.

Maybe ten seconds had passed and there were three large-caliber bullets in the bear. He was down but still moving a little.

"Put one more in him, Steve."

I was ready for that command this time. The .325 kicked my shoulder again, but I didn't really feel it. All I felt was awe and disbelief. *Had it really happened? Was there really a massive heap of dark fur lying lifeless in the grass behind the old tire? Did I do this deed? Yes, I did! Wow!*

While I kept the scope on the bear, Dale watched him for a half-minute before turning and looking at our cameraman with an expression that asked, "Did you get it?" Lindsey could tell Dale was curious and gave him the okay sign. Dale's subsequent smile and thumbs-up to the camera told us he was a satisfied guide with a satisfied hunter. It was the outcome that he'd worked hard for and that I'd dreamed about.

As the reality of the kill settled in, we sat for another five minutes and carefully watched the bear. I took an extra bullet out of my coat pocket and loaded it into the clip. I was taking no chances.

Lindsey took the opportunity to make sure the entire set-up and kill were recorded. He scrolled through a few scenes and then announced it was all there. We high-fived and celebrated the fact that we had not only experienced the live version of the hunt but also captured the event on video.

I can't put into words how glad and thankful I felt that our host had arranged for my hunt and for Lindsey to be here to document this incredible adventure.

Happy guide, happy hunter

We climbed down the other side of the rocky dome more carefully than we had climbed up. None of us wanted to break our body or our gear, especially the guns and camera. Feeling the pain of his recent fall on the rocks, Lindsey carefully went ahead of us to the beach, walked about thirty yards toward the old tire, and then turned around to film the guide and hunter leaving the large rocks. This meant he had his back to the bear. He was certainly a trusting soul. When my eyes

Leaving our setup site

weren't watching where I was stepping, they were fixed on the bear to make sure it didn't move.

I stepped where Dale stepped as we descended the outcropping. To be safely on the beach was a welcomed change. The ninety-yard, uphill walk to the bear felt like a mile as my boots slipped in the loose sand and gravel. On my way to poke the trophy of a lifetime in its eye with the end of my barrel to make absolutely sure he had expired, I thought, *What if the bear is just addled and decides to wake up when I'm standing over him? Do I really want to be that close?*

When I got within five yards of the bear, I stopped to watch his chest area for any motion. I couldn't believe how massive his body was. He was lying belly down, and it appeared that the top of his back was almost to my waistline. Unbelievable! Before I touched such a mammoth animal in its eye with the end of the rifle barrel, I decided it would be a good idea to slide the safety off and carefully suspend my finger over the trigger. If he as much as twitched I could touch off a shot and then run like the wind into Dale's arms (if he wasn't already holding Lindsey).

All the worry was for naught. The bear didn't move when I poked him.

For the next twenty minutes, we studied the brownie's features. The two-inch-long canines in his mouth numbered three instead of four. Something had taken one on the upper-right side of his jaw—perhaps another bear or simply old age. His fur was dense from head to toe except around the scar on his hip. The most amazing and chill-inducing features were the long, sharp, dark claws that protruded from his nearly eight-inch-wide pads on his feet. I didn't want to think about the damage that such a deadly set of lengthy thorns could render to human flesh. Just holding one of them up for a picture was a bit unsettling.

Ready to fire...and run!

It took all three of us to turn the bear on its back for examining and then back on its belly for pictures. It was hard work moving nearly a thousand pounds of lifeless bear. I silently wondered how in the world we were going to get it into the skiff. Before I had a chance to ask, Dale informed us that we'd leave him on the beach and come back very early the next morning with the entire hunting party. We'd work as a team to remove the boar's cape and head.

While I was relieved we wouldn't be lifting the body into the skiff, I questioned leaving him on the beach overnight. Dale smiled and assured me that the beast would still be right where we'd leave him when we returned bright and early the next morning. Our guide had been down this road before, and I had no reason to doubt his words.

Not long before sunset, Dale climbed over the rocks, got the skiff, and brought it around to the kill site. We had at least a half-hour ride back to *Surveyor*. We loaded our guns and gear into the boat and motored away from the beach. From my seat in the skiff, I turned to look back at my bear at the edge of the grass near the old tire. Several thoughts passed through my head.

Wait till Annie hears about this.

I can't wait till our host learns that the trip has yielded such a memory.

Mom and Dad are gonna be grateful that I haven't been mauled.

Sure hope something doesn't decide to make dinner out of my bear tonight.

I wonder if Jason connected this evening.

Lori's gonna smile when the skiff circles the boat at full speed.

It's day two of my dream hunt in Alaska…a day "two" remember for sure!

Pause for the claws

Sitting on a dream

26

The Cape Crew

It was around nine at night when we saw the interior lights of *Surveyor* in the cove. At about 200 yards out, Dale twisted the throttle wide open to do the traditional, post-kill, high-speed circle around her. Only Lori would hear the signal because Alex, Jason, and our host hadn't yet returned.

When they finally motored up to the platform at the aft of the big boat and came aboard, they knew by the looks on our faces that a bear was down. After the congratulatory greetings and a short retelling of the hunt, we headed to the galley to enjoy another "gotta just push through" dinner. After the meal, we watched the footage of the kill on the boat's TV. I was especially glad our host got to see the playback of the Tennessee boys experiencing the thrill of a successful hunt he'd arranged.

Before we went to our bunks, Dale announced that it would be a very early skiff ride to the beach where the tagged bear waited to be cut and caped. He suggested that everyone enjoy a simple breakfast and be ready to go just after sunrise. No one protested. I appreciated the corporate excitement about seeing my bear.

When *Surveyor*'s lights went out, I was staring again at the darkness over my bunk with a whole string of thoughts scrolling through my mind like ads on a bank marquee.

It's definitely too late to call Annie on the satellite phone. It would take her a week to get over a phone call at two in the morning. Maybe I can call her before we head out to cape the bear.

I wonder if she's heard anything about Dad.

What if the bear never turned broadside? Could have been a totally different ending to this day.

Dale sure knows his stuff.

That .325 is dandy. There's a grandson who's gonna love that gun.

Wish Jason had seen a shooter.

Sure is nice to not be answering emails.

Today is Tuesday, and I'm tagged out. Seven days of Alaska left with no pressure. Bring on the fishin'! Awesome—just awesome!

I don't think I should eat again until Friday.

Then my lights went out.

I woke up Wednesday morning with hopes that I could go topside with the satellite phone and give Annie a quick call, but it didn't happen. A quick breakfast and prepping to head back to the bear consumed the first thirty minutes. The next thing I knew we were boarding the skiffs and on our way.

The cape crew, left to right: Jason, our host, Steve, Lindsey, Dale, Alex

Just as Dale had assured us, the bear was still there and unharmed by any local scavengers. I wondered how much our "marking" on the ground around him the evening before had contributed to his

It takes a team to move a mountain

untouched condition—or was it the prayer I'd whispered? I assumed I'd never know and was just grateful the boar wasn't torn up during the night.

Before the process of caping began, Lindsey directed a photo opportunity. It took four strong men to manhandle the body of the bear into a position that would be perfect for pictures. We were almost in a sweat as we finally hunkered down behind the nearly thousand-pound body and posed as a group for some shots. Amazingly, five of us were able to fit shoulder to shoulder behind the length of the bear. That particular shot especially reveals how long he was.

Lindsey wanted some solo shots with just me and the beast as well as some close-ups with its intimidating claws in front of my face. And of course, we had to get Alex to take a few pictures of the two of us behind the bear in a nail-biting pose.

With the photo session complete, Dale and Alex put their knives to the cape. They worked together like a well-oiled machine as they "undressed" the bear. The rest of us served as assistants and followed their orders when they needed someone to sit on a leg or pull on the hide as they carefully and skillfully slid their razor-sharp knives under the skin. Their goal was to not slice through the hide so that the skin wouldn't have slits.

I'd used my bare hands to pull on the hide, and I noticed they now had a coating of grease that I wasn't sure I would ever get off. I mentioned it to Dale and learned that bear grease has had many uses through the centuries, including waterproofing, cooking, oiling guns, lubricating mechanical parts, and making dish soap, candles, and skin ointment. The grease on my hands was so heavy and thick I was sure it could have been used to grease the axles on my utility trailer at home.

A little more than an hour after they started cutting, Dale and Alex had removed the entire cape and head as one piece and set it aside in the thick grass behind the old tire. The only thing left was a huge, creamy-white, headless, ungutted carcass that would provide much-needed sustenance for the area eagle population. Dale said, "When we pass by the carcass again during the week, you can expect to see dozens of eagles picking it clean. They're the cleanup crew." Then he jokingly added, "You'll also see a bunch of eagles just sitting on the beach because they'll be so full they can't fly!"

The traditional wearing of the cape

With the knives wiped clean and our gear put away in the skiff, Dale announced that there was one thing left to do. I wasn't aware that I would be involved in yet another tradition. As the hunter, I was about to be "blessed" with the wearing of the cape.

Our guide and his assistant grinned as they walked up to the cape and then called me to join them. Dale asked me to turn away from them, facing the bay. Then they picked up the nine-foot-long cape and slowly wrapped it around my shoulders. I couldn't believe how heavy it was.

At about a hundred pounds, the freshly removed hide hung almost to the ground on each side of my body. I was straining just to stand. Then Dale said in a ritualistic tone, "It's time for your ceremonial walk to the skiff with your kill." Then they looked at Lindsey and said, "Roll film!"

I could barely walk down the incline of the gravel beach under the weight of the cape without my knees buckling. It was a long trip to the water's edge. When I got there, Lindsey said, "Uh, Steve, I need another take!"

I heard laughter. My voice was weak as I said, "Are you serious?"

"Yep. Gotta have some 'B' roll."

I looked back up to the old tire and mumbled as I began the climb. I was breathing heavily when I got to the edge of the grass and turned around.

"You'd better make this take count 'cause I can't do it a third time!"

My companions were having a party at the expense of my back, legs, shoulders, and sweat glands. But I was loving every minute of the challenge. At one point I thought, *A bear must have thought up this ritual, 'cause it sure feels like revenge!*

Bear coat!

Dale and Alex lifted the cape off my shoulders, folded it inside out, and put it in the skiff. We all climbed into the boats and backed away from the beach. As we did, I took one last look at the site where the climactic part of a longtime wish had come true. I felt a strange mixture of emotions. There was joy that I'd been blessed with an incredible bear hunt and a sobering awareness that the experience had changed from a dream to a memory. I would forever remember that stretch of Alaskan beach.

27

The Satellite Phone Call

When we returned to *Surveyor* just before noon, the first thing Lindsey and I did after helping get the bear cape on board, cleaning up, and storing our gear was to take the satellite phone to the upper deck to call home. Lindsey went first, and when my turn came to make the call, my hands shook with excitement as I punched in the long string of numbers. The anticipation of hearing my sweet wife's voice and breaking the good news to her about the bear was overwhelming.

As I waited for the call to process, I thought of how amazing it was that the technology I held in my hand would allow me to connect to a single landline in a house nearly three thousand miles away. I also thought of how comforting it was to know it was on board in case one of us got badly hurt and needed a floatplane. Thankfully, Lindsey skirted that need when he fell, but we had another week to enjoy in the remote Alaskan wilderness. I quickly prayed that we wouldn't have to make that kind of call.

Suddenly, I heard a click in the earpiece followed by "Hello?" Annie's voice was music to my ears. I assumed the question in her tone was due to the unfamiliar information the caller ID provided. Before she could dismiss the call as another telemarketer, I said, "Hey, Babe! Steve here!"

It had been three days of total silence from me, a silence that she hadn't had to deal with since I hunted elk for a week in Montana. We weren't used to not communicating for that long. Her response sounded very happy.

"Hey there! *Way* over there! Are you back in Sitka already?"

"Not yet. We have seven more days to go."

Her tongue-in-cheek response was pure Annie. "Ahhh, poor thing." Then she asked, "Do you have cell service?"

"No, I'm using the guide's satellite phone. I'm standing on the top deck of his boat outside the pilothouse looking at some incredible scenery. I wish you could see it with your own eyes. It's absolutely heavenly."

I could tell when Annie spoke that she was relieved to hear my upbeat tone. "I have no doubt the scenery is ringing your bell. I'd like to see it with you too. Sounds like you're having a good time. How's the hunt going?"

My heart raced as I answered because I had waited a lot of hours to tell her the news. "Well, yesterday evening I had an awesome moment."

"Yes?"

"We got into a big brownie—and I'm not talking about dessert. He was huge and heavy. I got myself a brown bear in Alaska. Can you believe it?"

I heard "Woo-hoo!" all the way from Tennessee followed by, "How awesome is that! Congratulations! I'm proud of you. I can't wait to tell the kids and the grandkids. They'll be so excited for you. I know you're thrilled."

"Yeah, I took the shot not long before sundown yesterday, and my insides still shake when I think about it. I can't wait to tell you the whole story…and show it to you too 'cause Lindsey recorded it all. For now, you can tell the fam that he weighed about a thousand pounds, and Dale Adams said the cape will measure over nine feet. I'll text a photo to you when we get back to Sitka."

I dreaded ending the call, but knowing that satellite minutes were a precious commodity, I told Annie that I loved her, that I appreciated her support of the trip, and that I'd call her later in the week to check in. Before we hung up, I asked, "Heard anything about Dad?"

"He's doing okay as far as I know. No news is good news."

I punched the off button on the phone and smiled with the thought that Annie was calling Nathan and Heidi to let them know about my bear. I knew they'd been as hopeful as I'd been that I'd get one. As I stood on the open deck and looked around at the eye-candy scenery out in the cove, I whispered a prayer of thanks for having such great news to tell Annie and my family. I also said a prayer for my ailing dad.

Calling home on the satellite phone

28

Beyond the Bear

With a tag already filled and a full week of Alaskan adventure still ahead of me, I looked forward to having no particular agenda to follow. I almost felt guilty for feeling so relaxed.

Although I would have enjoyed more days with a gun in hand in pursuit of a brown, there was plenty to do beyond the bear kill that would add to my inventory of great memories to take home. The following short descriptions are just a few of my favorites on the list.

- Almost every morning, Lindsey and I helped retrieve and empty the shrimp and crab pots, freshen the bait, and then take the pots back out to the honey-hole sites where the fishing was good. The two hours of constant movement required to complete the job gave me a new appreciation for those whose livelihoods are made on the big waters catching seafood. God bless them every one.
- We thoroughly enjoyed riding in the skiff for hours at a time with Alex as he motored around the various bays and inlets scouting for bear while Dale, Jason, and our host went hunting elsewhere. We were able to see a lot more of the seemingly endless miles of beach in the area. One especially intriguing land formation on Chichagof Island that we saw more than once was the shoreline that a lot of folks refer to as the

Boardwalk. It's a straight-line beach that stretches north to south for maybe fifteen miles. Scouting for bear in a skiff along the entire distance would take a whole day.

- On Thursday, we motored by the beach where I took my bear. We didn't go in close for the sake of not spooking another boar that might be walking the beach, but we were able to glass it from a distance. Sure enough, there were eagles by the dozens in the trees above the carcass, and as many sitting on the ground close to it either too full to lift off or waiting their turn to chow down. We could also see several eagles sitting on the skeleton picking at the remains of the bear flesh. I felt good about having been responsible for giving such a large number of our national birds a hearty meal.
- We had a very sobering and unforgettable moment navigating a quarter-mile-long, narrow strait during an outgoing tide. We needed to pass through it to get to an area to scout, and the view of the swirling waters from the very low vantage point of a skiff was ominous. As we skirted what appeared to be a whirlpool that resembled a giant version of bathwater twisting into a drain, it seemed that the water had a noticeable, round indentation that spanned about fifty yards. I was overjoyed that the skiff had a motor powerful enough to push us by the swirl and that our young friend at the controls had steady enough nerves and plenty of experience to navigate through such a chaotic passage. When we got beyond it to calmer waters, I breathed a sigh of relief and looked at Lindsey. His eyes were as big as fried eggs. We both hoped our return to *Surveyor* later that evening wouldn't be so risky. As it turned out, we went back another way—but I'm not sure it was any safer!

After the tense skiff ride through the "seriously dented" waters, we continued on for several hours, scouting some spectacular coves and a few smaller islands. About forty-five minutes before sundown, Alex announced that he hadn't planned to risk taking the skiff back through the fast-moving tide during the black of night. Instead, we would

Whirlpool alley—yikes!

beach the boat at the end of a cove and carry our gear through the thick timber, over a good-sized hill, and out to a cove on the other side. He'd arranged with Dale to pick us up there in the other skiff after he took Jason and our host to *Surveyor*.

I've been in some dense forests, especially in Colorado and Montana, but when we went behind the wall of huge timber that lined the cove and started into the deep shadows, I was stunned. What I saw ahead of me looked like growth that had been fertilized with steroids. The thick trees were only a foot or two apart, and the underbrush was tangled and tough to press through. The ground was soft and peppered with shin-deep holes that were hard to avoid because they were covered with soft moss and spruce needles.

It was near dark when we entered the timber. I kept thinking it looked like a place bears would live. Knowing they like to feed in the evening, I couldn't dismiss the thought that if there were hungry brown boars in the vicinity, they would have a three-course meal to enjoy. There were also sows with cubs to think about. I tried not to go there.

Because Alex had younger legs than Lindsey and me, he set a challenging pace up the hill. My lungs burned as I struggled to stay in the middle of the trio of hikers. I felt good about where I was in the line. I figured if there was a bear encounter, either the front man or the back man would be picked off first. Then somehow Lindsey got ahead of me, and suddenly I felt vulnerable.

Catch and consume

After half an hour of climbing up switchbacks and through dense underbrush, we finally dropped down a hillside to the shore. But there was no beach. The forest went all the way to the edge of the water. We found a small piece of soil and stayed there for more than an hour until we heard a skiff coming up the little inlet. It was a glorious sound! I wondered how in the world Dale would know which narrow cove we were in. Then I remembered he and Alex did this all the time. Plus, they want to get back to Lori's dinner as much as Lindsey and I did.

Another wonderful privilege that the trip provided was some rod-and-reel fishing. Alex was always ready to take Lindsey and me into some awesome inlets as well as bigger waters where we could drop a line. Using spinner lures and other types of artificial bait, we caught plenty of quillbacks, black sea bass, and rock fish to add to the table fare. We fished until our arms were weak and limp as wet noodles. The pay-off was hearing Dale say, "Gotta just push through" at the dining table.

There is one other thing to mention that occupied some of our time during the trip. It involves a gift I wanted to make for the man who had earned my respect doing the job I'd dreamed of doing so many years earlier. I wanted to offer him a sample of my work. Lindsey agreed to help me write and record a song for him.

Several times throughout the ten days as we got ready to go hunting, we heard Dale sing his "Big Brown Bear" ditty. The distinct melody he used sounded like a good start to a full-length song. I suggested to Lindsey that we build on it, adding some verses and a chorus.

We wanted the song to be a surprise. It wasn't easy to isolate ourselves on the boat, but we did. The best place was in the pilothouse. While Dale, Jason, and our host were on the final two afternoon and evening hunts, Lori worked below and Alex did various jobs, including prepping the cape for shipment. As they were occupied, Lindsey and I wrote the lyrics and expanded on Dale's melody. Using the Garage Band software on his iPad, Lindsey recorded a drum track, percussion tracks, and the bass line. Then he added a live track with the nylon-string guitar Dale's son, Ben, loaned to us. The only place to sing the vocal was outside on the top deck where the skiff crane was located. I stood watch as Lindsey used his headphones and sang into the iPad microphone.

Lindsey singing in God's great studio

Because of Lindsey's engineering and recording skills, he was able to create a very professional-sounding track with the iPad's easy-to-use software. His strong vocal fit the song style, and we looked forward to letting Dale hear it. Then I had yet another idea. Why not use the hunt footage we had to create a music video?

I had a laptop with me that had video-editing software. I quietly sat in the pilothouse putting different scenes into the timeline of the editing program. The feature of the video was Dale in his element. We included my bear, the kill, the cape crew, as well as the body-crunching "wearing of the cape" tradition they'd put me through.

By the time Sunday night came, we were ready to debut the three-minute movie. It was a hit—at least to everyone on board! Lindsey and I enjoyed Dale's big smile as he heard his name in the song. Below is the lyric.

Big Brown Bear

Big brown bear, big brown bear
He knows where they are, he'll take you there
Way up north to the Last Frontier
He can help you find a big brown bear

Big brown bear, big brown bear
He'll get you one with thick, dark hair
The wind and tide, they never play fair
But he'll push through for a big brown bear

Stovepipe nose, washtub head
Big ol' stud, Alaska fed
Hit 'im once, hit 'im again
Hit 'im till you see Dale Adams grin

Big brown bear, big brown bear
Coal-black eyes—can you feel his stare?
Listen to your guide, no need to be scared
And you'll be wearin' that big brown bear[3]

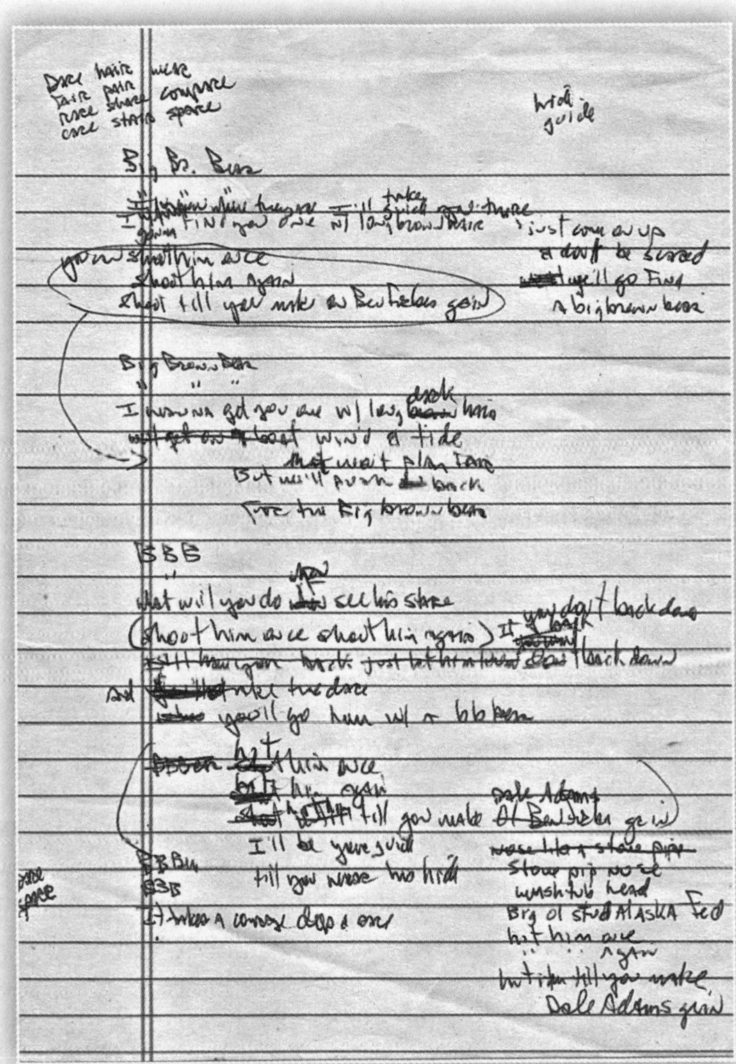

guide

just come on up
don't be scared
you'll go find
a big brown bear

Big Brown Bear

wind & tide

But we'll bring back

BBB

What will you do see his stare

(shoot him once shoot him again)

you'll go home w/ a bb bear

till you make gr in

I'll be your guide

till you wear his hide

Stove pipe nose
washtub head

hit him once
again

Dale Adams grin

Original lyric scribbling

29

Heading Home

My first journey into the Last Frontier as a hunter was about to come to a close. I heard the echo of what my first guide, Kenneth Bledsoe, had said to me back in the 1960s: "The hunt is over." I hadn't wanted to hear him say that in West Virginia all those years ago, and I didn't want to hear it echo in Alaska now. But we had a schedule to keep.

The four of us Lower Forty-Eighters had a flight departure out of Sitka at dawn on May 21. We decided as a group to get back to the dock on May 20 to make sure we wouldn't miss it. Dale agreed to accommodate us but suggested we not pull anchor until after the matinee hunt on May 19. He wanted to give Jason one more chance to take a bear. His commitment to the cause was appreciated, and no one protested.

As the trio of hunters returned from the final hunt, I was hoping they'd circle *Surveyor* in a victory lap, but it didn't happen. Jason obviously wanted to cap off the trip with a big bear, but he said leaving Alaska with a full clip meant only one thing—he'd have to come back and try it again. It was a plan every hunter smiled at.[4]

After teaming up with Alex to hoist the two skiffs back onto their bunks on the top deck of *Surveyor*, Dale announced that Lori had dinner ready for us. Afterward, we'd set sail, taking the "big water" route through the night as we headed south instead of backtracking the inland route we'd taken in. This meant we would be outside the protection of the

Wishing I could stay

islands and in dark seas with swells that could create quite a roller-coaster ride. With that in mind, it was necessary to make sure everything was tied down securely.

Not long before midnight, Dale started the mighty Cummins diesel. The voyage out of the inland bay to the big seas took about forty-five minutes, which gave me time to imagine what could happen in the deep of night on the rolling waters.

What if the engine stops?

What if a heavy storm surprises us and pushes us into the rocks?

What if we capsize and sink?

What if the radios go silent?

What if Dale passes out all alone in the pilothouse while everyone else is asleep?

As the what-ifs tested my faith, I silently reminded myself once more, *There is no grace for borrowed sorrow*. I had to let go of the worry and get my mind on something else. I decided to do something proactive, so I joined Dale in the pilothouse to keep him company and help him stay alert. Besides, it would be the best seat in the floating home to see the sights that *Surveyor's* powerful lights could provide on the big waves.

For me, it was indeed a topsy-turvy ride, but Dale was obviously used to it. He seemed quite relaxed at the wheel. His confidence fed my comfort, and after a while I began to enjoy the rock and roll. Watching him constantly monitor the radar and other navigational devices was entertaining enough, but hearing some of his stories made the night voyage even more memorable. One of my favorites wasn't about a hunt. Instead, he told me about an antihunting activist he'd met at his company's display booth at a huge hunting show.

"This lady walked up to my table. When she started talking, I knew immediately she was anti-everything when it came to hunting. She was, pun intended, 'loaded for bear' as she demeaned my vocation. Then, with a frightening scowl on her face, she asked a question that was well rehearsed and designed to trap unsuspecting hunters and guides. 'Do you eat the bear meat or do you just leave it to rot?'"

In the dim light of the pilothouse I saw Dale slide his hand over his mouth, showing that after all the time that had passed since that encounter, he was still feeling the emotions that had risen in him. He said he quickly considered how he could defend himself as well as all his comrades in the guiding industry.

"I thought about lying to her and saying, 'Yes, ma'am, I eat every last ounce.' My conscience wouldn't let me do that. Then I had a thought that I consider now to be a stroke of genius. I looked square into her furious eyes and tenderly told her the truth.

"Ma'am, the winters in Alaska are very hard on our eagle population. Every year we lose too many of our precious national birds to starvation. It gets so bad they'll kill and eat innocent seagulls, ravens, magpies—and even each other—to survive. The waters are frozen, which means there are no fish to catch and eat. By the time bear season arrives in the spring, the poor eagles are emaciated and weak. I suppose we could take the bear meat with us when we kill one, but we prefer to leave the carcass—everything but the head and cape—right there on the beach for the eagles. When I see dozens of ravenous bald eagles clustered around a thousand-pound offering of nutritious, life-sustaining meat, I can almost hear their expressions of thanks. When they fly by, they seem to tip their wings in a show of gratitude. Ma'am, we do it for the eagles.'"

I could see Dale smiling in the glow of the computer screens that sat in front him. "I meant every word of what I said, and when I finished talking she looked at me for a few seconds. Then she reached across the table, hugged me, and cried. I sure didn't expect that reaction. I bet she didn't either!"

I congratulated Dale for helping someone appreciate the reality of the cycle of life that is so clearly displayed in nature. We both agreed that, unfortunately, it's a truth that is too often buried under urban thinking that tends to humanize animals and animalize humans.

As we sailed on, my intention to stay awake through the entire night to provide Dale with company was defeated by the lulling effect of the boat. I drifted off to sleep in the pilothouse about three in the morning and didn't wake up until we were about an hour from Sitka. The sun was coming up, and the waters were calm.

As I sat up and looked around at the shorelines on both sides, I whispered a prayer of thanks for the power and durability of the big engine that had worked flawlessly for the previous six hours. Then I thanked Dale for his endurance at the wheel of *Surveyor*. He gave me a "you're welcome" grin and rubbed his face with both hands. It was clear he was tired, but thanks to Lori and hot coffee, he was still fully able to take us on to the dock.

I got a whiff of the brew coming from below and headed to the cup cabinet. I found that Alex was up. When I asked him if it was always exciting to get back to town after ten work-packed days away, he nodded and said yes. But the thrill of the return was tempered by the work to be done. The crew would replenish the supplies, greet a new group of hunters in a couple of days, sail north, and do it all again.

I sighed and said, "It's a tough job, but someone has to do it. If only there were more of me…"

As Dale slowly snugged his big boat up to the dock, Alex jumped onto the wooden walkway and wrapped the mooring ropes around the bollards at the bow and stern. While they worked together, I thought of my cell phone that I hadn't yet turned on. Within a minute of getting a signal the emails started pouring in. I didn't bother to check them at the moment because I needed to help unload everyone's gear. I stepped

Safe after our early morning return to Sitka

out on the dock, and at that very moment my cell phone rang. I hadn't heard the familiar tone for ten days.

I tapped the green button, put the phone to my ear, and said, "Hello," with a jovial tone. I heard someone say my name, and it was obviously spoken through tears. I immediately recognized my sister's voice.

"Steve?"

"Yes, Jeannie?"

"Steve, they just took Dad to the hospital. I'm on my way there now. Where are you?"

My heart sank. "I'm in Sitka, Alaska. We just got back to the dock from the bear hunt. Do you know how serious Dad's condition is?"

"No. Mom called and said the EMTs had to go to the house and take him to the emergency room. Apparently he was having a really hard time breathing." Jeannie struggled to speak as she told me that she was beginning the ninety-minute drive from her home in Ohio to our hometown in West Virginia. I encouraged her to be careful and tried to comfort her, but it wasn't much consolation for her to know I was still in Alaska.

"I fly out in the morning. As soon as I get back to Tennessee, I'll head to West Virginia. Call Annie or me if you get an update. The signal here is good." We prayed for our dad and said goodbye.

I was so stunned by the news that I stood motionless on the dock. Everyone was carrying gear bags and supplies to Dale's truck. I finally shook myself and told our host about the call I'd just received. He was very sympathetic and said he would pass the news on to his wife when he called her so she could add her prayers to my family's. I was grateful. I told Lindsey about Dad, and he too showed great concern. Eventually the rest of our hunting party was aware of the news and offered their prayers.

As the day went on, I thought about the timing of my sister's shocking call. If it had been at any other time during the ten days, she wouldn't have been able to connect with me so easily. There were not enough words to say sufficient thanks to God for the fact that I was back in cell phone range when she'd called. I was grateful to be able to pray for the greatest man I've ever known in his hour of distress.

Later that morning, I got another call from Jeannie. I was relieved to learn that Dad was stable and in good hands at Pleasant Valley Hospital. His battle with congestive heart failure was fierce, but he seemed to be winning at the moment.

I was eager to get back to Tennessee and then to West Virginia to see my father again.

We stayed overnight once more at the Westmark in Sitka and were up well before daylight the next morning to ride in Dale's truck to the airport. It was an emotional farewell. Though I'd been around the team a relatively short time, I felt as if I'd known them all my life. That's how much they made me feel like family.

After our hunting party checked our duffel bags and rifle cases at the ticket counter, we gathered with Dale in the back corner of the bag claim area next to another huge bear in a display case! It was a full mount of a trophy taken by none other than Dale Adams. We were just beginning to enjoy hearing the story behind the taking of the big brownie when we were interrupted by the announcement that it was time to go through the security checkpoint.

We shook Dale's hand and said farewell. When it came my turn, I slipped my hand into his strong, sea-worn hand, and the overwhelming thought hit me that fifty years before that moment, I had started dreaming about being with a guide on a bear hunt in Alaska—and it had happened!

When the Delta flight lifted off the ground, I watched the town of Sitka disappear in the distance. As it did, I started dreaming about going back someday to hunt bear in the great state of Alaska.

Epilogue

Like a Mighty Eagle

When I returned to Tennessee, I hugged my dear wife, Annie, had dinner with my entire family, and gave a pictorial and video report on my trip. I did some quick catch-up in our home office, and the next morning I took off for the six-and-a-half-hour drive to West Virginia. It would be the first of many trips I'd make from late May until Thanksgiving so I could be with Dad and help Mom as she cared for him.

Dad endured several painful procedures through the long months, hoping they would help his body get stronger. Instead, he grew weaker. He turned 89 in August and made it through Thanksgiving. Two days later, on November 28, at about one in the afternoon, his journey through time came to an end.

Along with being an incredible husband for sixty-eight years to my mother, Lillian, he was an outstanding dad. He was a Navy veteran, a highly respected citizen in his hometown, and a faithful friend and neighbor.

My mom called him PJ, Jeannie and I called him Dad, our children called him Sweet Pappy, but to most people in his area he was simply known as Preacher Chapman. Next to the joy of caring for his family, being a preacher-pastor at the Church of God was the role that gave him the most satisfaction and sense of purpose. He was a fine minister.

Along with his passion for studying the Bible, Dad had a special love for gospel music. He promoted concerts in his home county and enjoyed writing songs. Many of us still sing the chorus of his song "It's Lookin' Up Time."

A mighty warrior!

It's lookin' up time, your redemption draweth nigh
It's lookin' up time, keep your eyes on the sky
He's coming that way, it may be today
Children, it's lookin' up time[5]

Another favorite was a short, humorous song that he was always willing and ready to sing.

When you get to heaven, you will likely view
Many smiling faces that will be a shock to you
But be very quiet, don't you even stare
'Cause they'll be just as shocked when they see you there[6]

The last song he worked on was with me. During one of his stays in the hospital, I was with him on a Sunday morning. Since he couldn't go to church, we had fellowship in his room. I was reading the Bible to him. When we came to 1 John 2, which starts with "My little children, I am writing these things to you so that you may not sin. And if anyone sins, we have an Advocate with the Father, Jesus Christ the righteous." Near the end of the chapter, in verse 28, it says, "Now, little children, abide in Him, so that when He appears, we may have confidence and not shrink away from Him in shame at His coming."

To further redeem the time spent confined to the hospital room, I suggested to Dad that we write a song that features these verses. We started exchanging ideas, and the lyric that was written is a statement especially directed to Dad's children, grandchildren, great-grandkids, and his great-great-grandchild.

When Jesus Appears

Oh my children, my children so dear
I write to remind you His coming is near
I'm praying that you will be faithful and true
So you won't be ashamed when Jesus appears
When Jesus appears, when Jesus appears
So you won't be ashamed when Jesus appears

Oh my children, my children so dear
I write to remind you, His mercy is near
When you fall in this race, you can trust in His grace
So you won't be ashamed when Jesus appears

Oh my children, my children so dear
I write to remind you, be of good cheer
How great is His love that washed you with blood
So you won't be ashamed when Jesus appears

When Jesus appears, when Jesus appears
So you won't be ashamed when Jesus appears[7]

Because Dad lived 89 years and 89 days, it was fitting that Psalm 89:1 be read at his graveside service. Considering the quality of his leadership as a family man and his deep passion for music, this reading was very special for our family.

> I will sing of the lovingkindness of the Lord forever;
> to all generations I will make known Your faithfulness
> with my mouth.

One final note about my dad. I was helping him stand up when his spirit departed for heaven. It was an incredible experience that I'll never forget. When I recall that amazing moment, I remember something I observed while in Alaska.

When we'd anchored close to shore, I enjoyed sitting on the aft deck and watching the eagles. They would perch in the top limbs of the nearby trees and wait for one of us to throw the carcasses of the freshly caught and cleaned fish in the water or for Alex to toss another string of fat overboard that he'd scraped off the bear cape as he prepared it for shipping.

When the free food would hit the water, the eagles would spread their powerful wings and lift off with amazing power and ease. Within seconds, they gained altitude and soared with grace. Recalling how they took to the air is the picture I see when I think of Dad lifting off on his flight to heaven.

With that imagery in mind, these words were written to honor the life and times of the greatest man I ever knew. I journey on today without him, but his memory inspires me to do all I can to be as good a guide for my family as he was for his.

I Held a Great Warrior

In honor of Paul J. Chapman
(August 31, 1926–November 28, 2015)

I held a great warrior when he died
When his spirit made the journey to the other side
It was like a mighty eagle just lifted off in flight
I held a great warrior when he died

He fought hard
He fought well
God knows how many souls he led away from hell
He was tired
To the bone
But I heard him singing 'bout the day that he'd go home

I don't know why I was chosen
To be there when he died
But I'll have no greater honor
As long as I live

With his life he showed me how to win the war
Fight every battle with the Sword of the Lord

I held a great warrior when he died
When his spirit made the journey to the other side
It was like a mighty eagle just lifted off in flight
I held a great warrior when he died[8]

Like a mighty eagle...

Notes

1. Lindsey Williams and Steve Chapman, "You Just Never Know," Really Big Bison Music, SESAC, Times & Seasons Music, BMI, 2014. Used by permission. All rights reserved.
2. Steve Chapman, "The Guide," Times & Seasons Music, BMI, 2001. Used by permission. All rights reserved.
3. Steve Chapman and Lindsey Williams with Lori Adams, "Big Brown Bear," Times & Seasons Music, Really Big Bison Music, SESAC, BMI, 2015. Used by permission. All rights reserved.
4. I learned during the writing of this story that Jason was heading back to Alaska to hunt a bear a second time. There's not a jealous bone in my body. Still later, I learned that Jason had gotten his bear. Congratulations to Jason and his hunting guide, Alex.
5. Paul J. Chapman, "It's Lookin' Up Time," Times & Seasons Music, 1996. Used by permission. All rights reserved.
6. Paul J. Chapman, "When You Get to Heaven," Times & Seasons Music, 1995. Used by permission. All rights reserved.
7. Paul J. Chapman and Steve Chapman, "When Jesus Appears," Times & Seasons Music, 2015. Used by permission. All rights reserved.
8. Steve Chapman, "I Held a Great Warrior When He Died," Times & Seasons Music, BMI, 2015. Used by permission. All rights reserved.

More Great Books by the Chapman Family

STEVE CHAPMAN

10 Ways to Prepare Your Son for Life
365 Things Every Hunter Should Know
Another Look at Life from a Deer Stand
Down Home Wit and Wisdom
Great Hunting Stories
A Look at Life from a Deer Stand
A Look at Life from a Deer Stand Gift Edition
A Look at Life from a Deer Stand Devotional
The Hunter's Devotional
A Look at Life from the Riverbank
A Sportsman's Call
Stories from the Deer Stand
The Tales Hunters Tell
Wasn't It Smart of God to...
With Dad on a Deer Stand
With Dad on a Deer Stand Gift Edition

ANNIE CHAPMAN

10 Ways to Prepare Your Daughter for Life
Letting Go of Anger
The Mother-in-Law Dance
Taking Back Your Life...One Thought at a Time

STEVE AND ANNIE CHAPMAN

52 Prayers for My Grandchild
The Hunter's Cookbook
I Love You and I Like You